U.S. Fish and Wildlife Service

Mourning Dove
Breeding Population Status, 2001

I0410834

MOURNING DOVE BREEDING POPULATION STATUS, 2001

DAVID D. DOLTON, U.S. Fish and Wildlife Service, Division of Migratory Bird Management, PO Box 25486 DFC, Denver, CO 80225-0486

REBECCA D. HOLMES, U.S. Fish and Wildlife Service, Division of Migratory Bird Management, Patuxent Wildlife Research Center, 11500 American Holly Dr., Laurel, MD 20708-4016

GRAHAM W. SMITH, U.S. Fish and Wildlife Service, Division of Migratory Bird Management, Patuxent Wildlife Research Center, 11500 American Holly Dr., Laurel, MD 20708-4016

Abstract: This report includes Mourning Dove Call-count Survey information gathered over the last 36 years within the conterminous United States. Trends were calculated for the most recent 2- and 10-year intervals and for the entire 36-year period. Between 2000 and 2001, the average number of doves heard per route decreased significantly in the Eastern and Central Management Units. No change was detected for the Western Unit. Over the most recent 10 and 36-year periods, significant declines were indicated for doves heard in the Central and Western Units. Additionally, in the Eastern Management Unit, a significant decline was detected over the most recent 10 years while there was no trend indicated over 36 years. In contrast, for doves seen over the 10-year period, a significant increase was found in the Eastern Unit while no trends were found in the Central and Western Unit. Over the 36-year period, no trend was found for doves seen in the Eastern and Central Units while a decline was indicated for the Western Unit.

The mourning dove (*Zenaida macroura*) is a migratory bird, thus, authority and responsibility for its management is vested in the Secretary of the Interior. This responsibility is conferred by the Migratory Bird Treaty Act of 1918, which, as amended, implements migratory bird treaties between the United States and other countries. Mourning doves are included in the treaties with Great Britain (for Canada) and Mexico. These treaties recognize sport hunting as a legitimate use of a renewable migratory bird resource. As one of the most abundant species in both urban and rural areas of North America, it is familiar to millions of people. Maintenance of mourning dove populations in a healthy, productive state is a primary management goal. To this end, management of doves includes assessment of population status, regulation of harvest, and habitat management. Call-count surveys are conducted annually in the 48 conterminous states by state and federal biologists to monitor mourning dove populations. The resulting information on status and trends is used by wildlife administrators in setting annual hunting regulations.

DISTRIBUTION AND ABUNDANCE

Mourning doves breed from the southern portions of Canada throughout the United States into Mexico, Bermuda, the Bahamas and Greater Antilles, and scattered locations in Central America (Fig. 1). Although some mourning doves winter throughout most of the breeding range, except for central Canada and the north-central U.S., the majority migrate south, wintering in the southern United States and south throughout most of Mexico and Central America to western Panama (Aldrich 1993, Mirarchi and Baskett 1994).

The mourning dove is one of the most widely distributed and abundant birds in North America (Peterjohn et al. 1994, Fig. 1). Although not known precisely, the fall population has been estimated to be about 475 million (Dunks et al. 1982, Tomlinson et al. 1988). However, as there is evidence of population decreases since this estimate was made from data collected in the 1970's, we believe that the mourning dove population has declined to slightly more than 400 million in the United States.

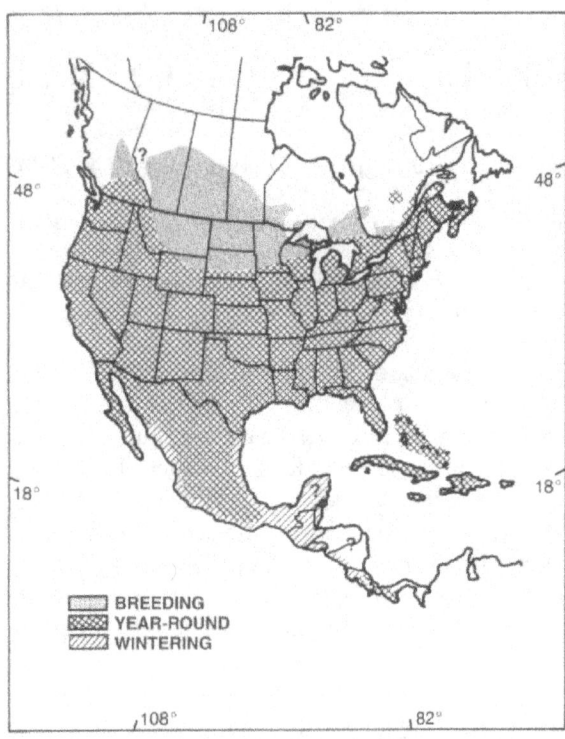

Fig. 1. Breeding and wintering ranges of the mourning dove (adapted from Mirarchi and Baskett 1994).

POPULATION MONITORING

The Mourning Dove Call-count Survey was developed to provide an annual index to population size (Dolton 1993). This survey is based on work by McClure (1939) in Iowa. Field studies demonstrated the feasibility of the survey as a method for detecting annual changes in mourning dove breeding populations (Foote and Peters 1952). In the United States, the survey currently includes more than 1,000 randomly selected routes, stratified by physiographic region. In Canada, 20 randomly selected routes are located in parklands and prairie. The total number of doves heard on each route is used to determine trends in populations and provides the basis for determining an index to population size during the breeding season. Indices for doves seen are also presented in this report, but only as supplemental information for comparison with indices of doves heard. Even though both the numbers of doves heard and seen are counted during the survey, they are recorded separately.

Within the United States, there are 3 zones that contain mourning dove populations that are largely independent of each other (Kiel 1959). These zones encompass the principal breeding, migration, and U.S. wintering areas for each population. As suggested by Kiel (1959), these 3 areas were established as separate management units in 1960 (Kiel 1961). Since that time, management decisions have been made within the boundaries of the Eastern (EMU), Central (CMU), and Western (WMU) Management Units (Fig. 2).

The EMU was further divided into 2 groups of states for analyses. States permitting dove hunting were combined into one group and those prohibiting dove hunting into another. Additionally, some states were grouped to increase sample sizes. Maryland and Delaware were combined; Vermont, New Hampshire, Maine, Massachusetts, Connecticut, and Rhode Island were combined to form a New England group. Due to its small size, Rhode Island, which is a hunting state, was included in this nonhunting group of states for analysis.

METHODS

The Call-count Survey

Each call-count route is usually located on secondary roads and has 20 listening stations spaced at 1-mile intervals. At each stop, the number of doves heard calling, the number seen, and the level of disturbance (noise) that impairs the observer's ability to hear doves are recorded. The number of doves seen while driving between stops is also noted.

Counts begin one-half hour before sunrise and continue for about 2 hours. Routes are run once between 20 May and 5 June. Intensive studies in the eastern United States (Foote and Peters 1952) indicated that dove calling is relatively stable during this period. Surveys are not made when wind velocities exceed 12 miles per hour or when it is raining.

Estimation of Population Trends

A population trend is defined as the ratio of the dove population in an area in one year to the population in the preceding year. For more than 2 years of data, the

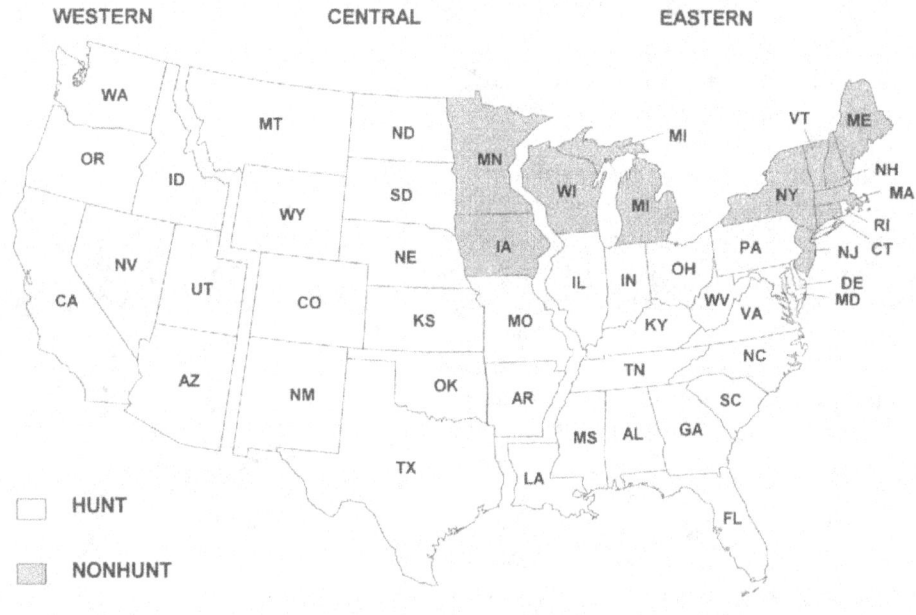

Fig. 2. Mourning dove management units with 2000 hunting and nonhunting states.

trend is expressed as an average annual rate of change. A trend was first estimated for each route by numerically solving a set of estimating equations (Link and Sauer 1994). Observer data were used as covariables to adjust for differences in observers' ability to hear or see doves. The reported sample sizes are the number of routes on which a given trend estimate is based. This number may be less than the actual number of routes surveyed for several reasons. The estimating equations approach requires at least 2 non-zero counts by at least one observer for a route to be used. Routes that did not meet this requirement during the interval of interest were not included in the sample size. State and management unit trends were obtained by calculating a mean of all route trends weighted by land area, within-route variance in counts, and density (mean numbers of doves counted on each route). Variances of state and management unit trends were estimated by using route trends and a statistical procedure known as bootstrapping (Geissler and Sauer 1990).

The annual change, or trend, for each area in doves heard over the most recent 2- and 10-year intervals and for the entire 36-year period were estimated. Additionally, trends in doves seen were estimated over the 10- and 36-year periods as supplemental information for comparison.

For purposes of this report, statistical significance was defined as $P<0.05$, except for the 2-year comparison where $P<0.10$ was used because of the low power of the test. Significance levels are approximate for states with less than 10 routes.

Estimation of Annual Indices

Annual indices show population fluctuations about fitted trends (Sauer and Geissler 1990). The estimated indices were determined for an area (state or management unit) by finding the deviation between observed counts on a route and those predicted on the route from the area trend estimate. These residuals were averaged by year for all routes in the area of interest. To adjust for variation in sampling intensity, residuals were weighted by the land area of the physiographic regions within each state. These weighted average residuals were then added to the fitted trend for the area to produce the annual index of abundance. This method of determining indices superimposes yearly variation in counts on the long-term fitted trend. These indices should provide an accurate representation of the fitted trend for regions that are adequately sampled by survey routes. Additionally, only data from within an area are incorporated into the area's index. Since the indices are adjusted for observer differences and trend, the index for an area may be quite different from the

3

actual count. In order to estimate the percent change from 2000 to 2001, a short-term trend (2 years) was calculated. The percent change estimated from this short-term trend analysis is the best estimator of annual change. Attempts to estimate short-term trends from the breeding population indices (which were derived from residuals of the long-term trends) will yield less precise results. The annual index value incorporates data from a large number of routes that are not comparable between the two years 2000 and 2001, i.e., routes not run by the same observers. Therefore, the index is much more variable than the trend estimate.

In a separate analysis, the mean number of doves heard calling per route in 2001 was calculated for each state or groups of states. In contrast to the estimated annual indices presented in Table 2 (which illustrate population changes over time based on the regression line), the estimated densities shown in Figs. 3, 7, and 11 illustrate the average *actual* numbers of doves counted in 2000 and 2001.

RESULTS

Eastern Management Unit

The Eastern Management Unit includes 27 states comprising 30% of the land area of the United States. Dove hunting is permitted in 18 states, representing 74% of the land area of the unit (Fig. 2).

2000-2001 Population Distribution.--North Carolina had one of the highest counts in the Nation with about 36 actual doves heard per route over the 2 years (Fig. 3). New York, Pennsylvania, New Jersey, and the New England states averaged < 10 per route. Georgia had slightly more than 20 doves heard per route while all other states had mean counts in the range of 10-20.

2000 to 2001 Population Changes.--A significant decrease was detected for the Unit. The average number of doves heard per route decreased 6.1% (Table 1). The population did not change significantly between years in the combined hunting states (-3.6%). The index for the combined nonhunting states did decrease significantly (16.2%).

The 2001 population index of 16.3 doves heard per route for the Unit, was above the predicted count

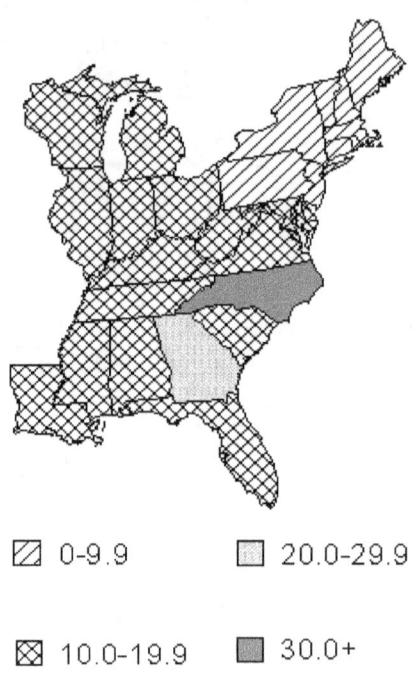

▨ 0-9.9		☐ 20.0-29.9	
▧ 10.0-19.9		▨ 30.0+	

Fig. 3. Mean number of mourning doves heard per route by state in the Eastern Management Unit, 2000-2001.

MEAN PER ROUTE

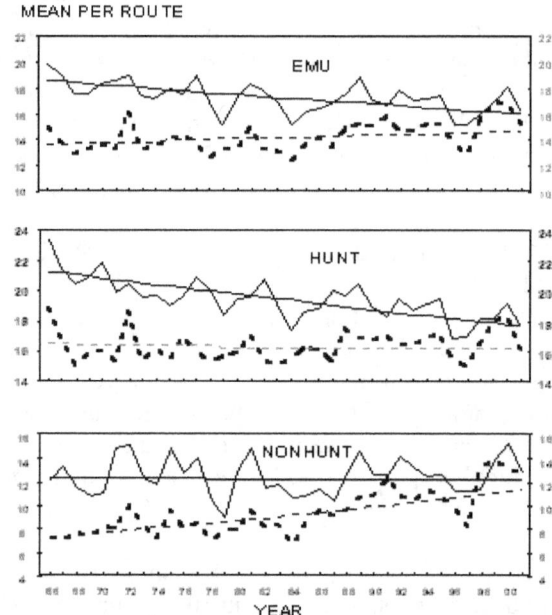

Fig. 4. Population indices and trends of breeding mourning doves in the Eastern Management Unit (EMU), combined EMU hunting states (HUNT), and combined EMU nonhunting states (NONHUNT), 1966-2001. Heavy solid line = doves heard; heavy dash line = doves seen; light solid and dash lines = predicted trends.

4

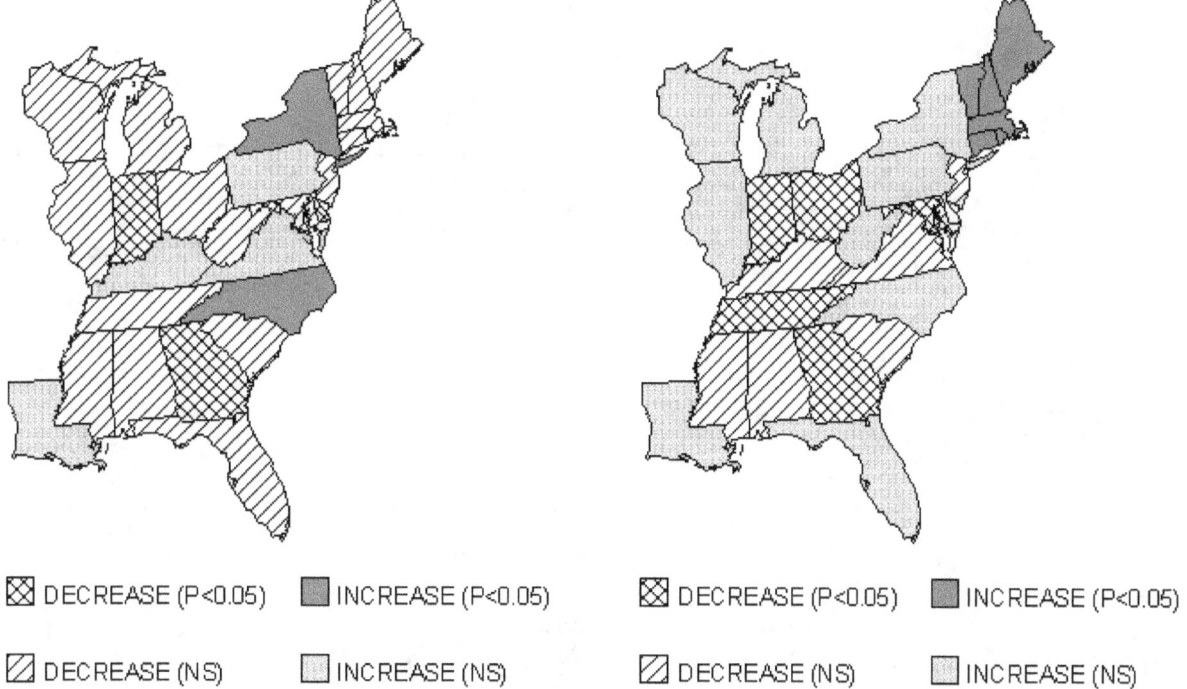

Fig. 5. Trends in number of mourning doves heard per route by state in the Eastern Management Unit, 1992-2001.

Fig. 6. Trends in the number of mourning doves heard per route by state in the Eastern Management Unit, 1966-2001.

based on the long-term estimate of 16.0 (Fig. 4, Table 2). In the hunting states, the index of 17.2 is essentially the same as the predicted estimate of 17.3, while in the nonhunting states, the index of 12.6 is above the predicted estimate of 12.0.

The population increased significantly in Delaware/ Maryland, Georgia, and West Virginia while it decreased in Tennessee, Michigan, and New Jersey (Table 1). No significant changes were detected for other states.

Population Trends: 10 and 36-year.--Analyses indicated significant declines over the most recent 10 and 36-year periods for the combined hunting (Table 1). No trend was found over either time period for the combined nonhunting states. For the Unit, there was a significant decline over 10 years and no trend [although a tendency toward a trend ($P<0.10$)] over the long term. Annual indices both for doves heard and seen are shown in Fig. 4. In contrast to doves heard, an analysis of doves seen indicated a significant increasing trend for the Unit and 2 groups of states over 10 years. No trend was detected over 36 years for the Unit or combined hunting states. For the

combined nonhunting states, no trend was detected in doves heard for both time periods while an analysis of doves seen showed a significant increasing trend over the 2 periods.

State population trends for doves heard are shown in Fig. 5 (10-year interval) and Fig. 6 (36-year interval) and Table 1). Over 10 years, increases were found for North Carolina and New York while Georgia and Indiana showed declines. Between 1966 and 2001, an increase was noted in New England, while a downward trend was noted in Delaware/Maryland, Georgia, Indiana, Ohio, and Tennessee.

Central Management Unit

The Central Management Unit consists of 14 states, containing 46% of the land area in the U.S. It has the highest population index of the 3 units. Within the unit, dove hunting is permitted in 12 states (Fig. 2).

2000-2001 Population.--Nebraska, North Dakota, and South Dakota had the highest actual average number of doves heard per route over the 2 years (28, 35, and 28, respectively) (Fig. 7). Historically, North Dakota

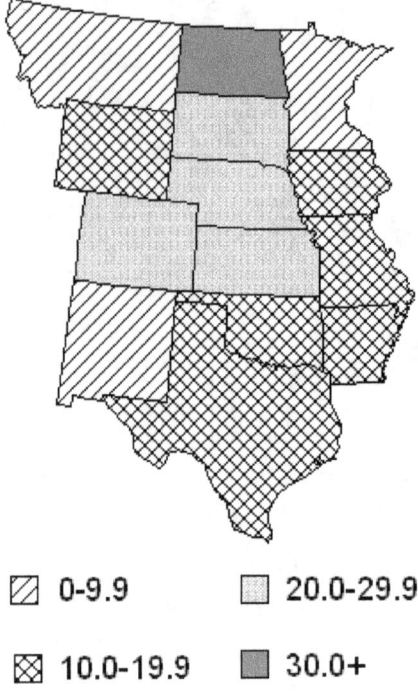

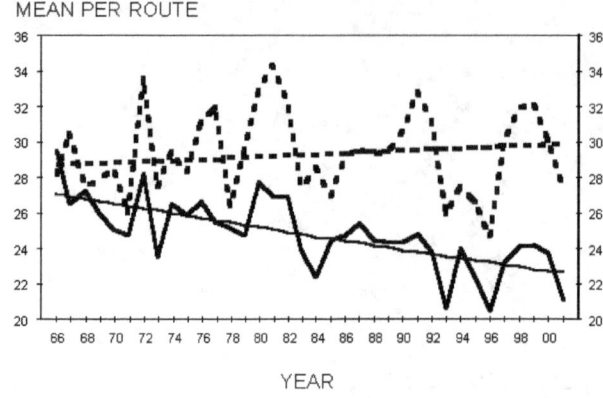

Fig. 8. Population indices and trends of breeding mourning doves in the Central Management Unit, 1966-2001. Heavy solid lines = doves heard; heavy dash line = doves seen. Light solid and dash lines = predicted trends.

⊘ 0-9.9	☐ 20.0-29.9
⊠ 10.0-19.9	■ 30.0+

Fig. 7. Mean number of mourning doves heard per route by state in the Central Management Unit, 2000-2001.

and Kansas often have the highest average counts in the Nation (Table 2). Minnesota, Montana, and New Mexico were the only states with less than 10 doves per route. The remaining states had intermediate values.

2000 to 2001 Population Changes.--The average number of doves heard per route in the Unit decreased significantly between the 2 years (-9.4%; Table 1). The 2001 index for the Unit of 22.1 doves heard per route is only slightly below the predicted long-term trend estimate of 22.7 (Fig. 8, Table 2).

The population increased significantly in New Mexico (Table 1). Significant decreases were found in Colorado, Kansas, Minnesota, Montana, North Dakota, and Wyoming.

Population Trends: 10 and 36-year.--A significant decline in doves heard was indicated for the Unit over both time periods (Table 1). Trends for doves seen were not significant for either time period. State trends over 10 years are illustrated in Fig. 9 and Table 1. Montana showed an increase while Missouri and Texas had declines during this time. Fig. 10

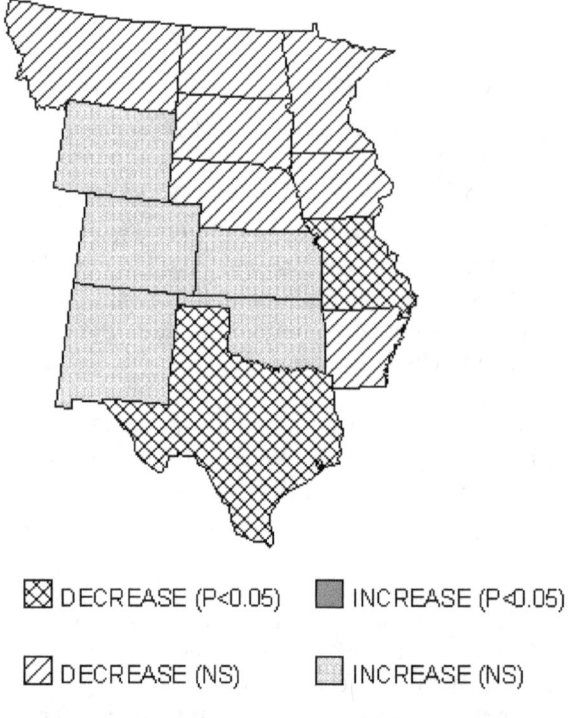

⊠ DECREASE (P<0.05)	■ INCREASE (P<0.05)
⊘ DECREASE (NS)	☐ INCREASE (NS)

Fig. 9. Trends in number of mourning doves heard per route by state in the Central Management Unit, 1992-2001.

portrays trends over 36 years. No significant upward trend was found in doves heard for any state, but a significant downward trend was found in Missouri (Table 1).

6

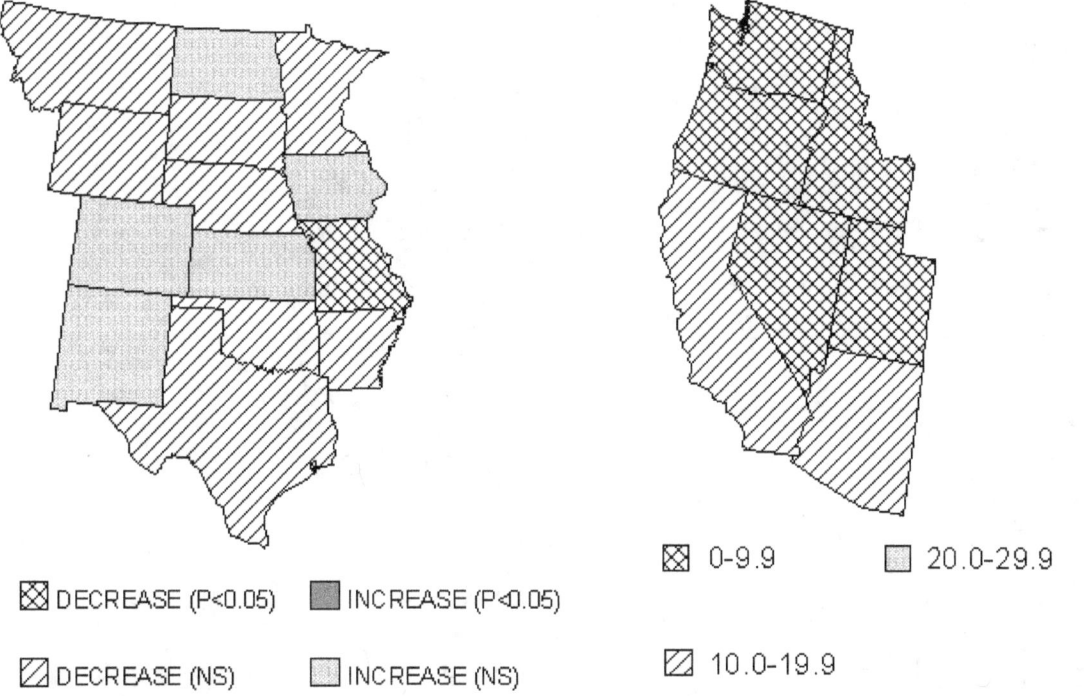

DECREASE (P<0.05)   INCREASE (P<0.05)

DECREASE (NS)   INCREASE (NS)

0-9.9   20.0-29.9

10.0-19.9

Fig. 10. Trends in mourning doves heard per route by state in the Central Management Unit, 1966-2001.

Fig. 11. Mean number of mourning doves heard per route by state in the Western Management Unit, 2000-2001.

Western Management Unit

Seven states comprise the Western Management Unit and represent 24% of the land area in the United States. All states within the unit permit mourning dove hunting.

2000-2001 Population Distribution.–Arizona and California averaged 12 and 11 actual doves heard per route, respectively (Fig. 11). The other states in the Unit averaged < 10 birds per route.

2000 to 2001 Population Changes.--The average number of doves heard per route did not change significantly between years, although the index decreased by 7.1% (Table 1). The 2001 population index of 8.5 doves heard per route is essentially the same as the predicted count of 8.4 based on the long-term estimate (Fig. 12, Table 2).

The number of doves heard per route increased significantly in Arizona (Table 1). Significant decreases were found in California, Idaho, Nevada, and Utah.

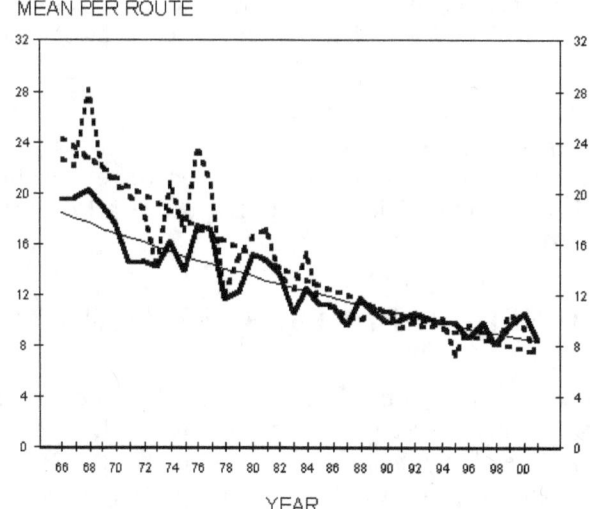

MEAN PER ROUTE

YEAR

Fig. 12. Population indices and trends of breeding mourning doves in the Western Management Unit, 1966-2001. Heavy solid line = doves heard; heavy dash line = doves seen; light solid and dash lines = predicted trends.

7

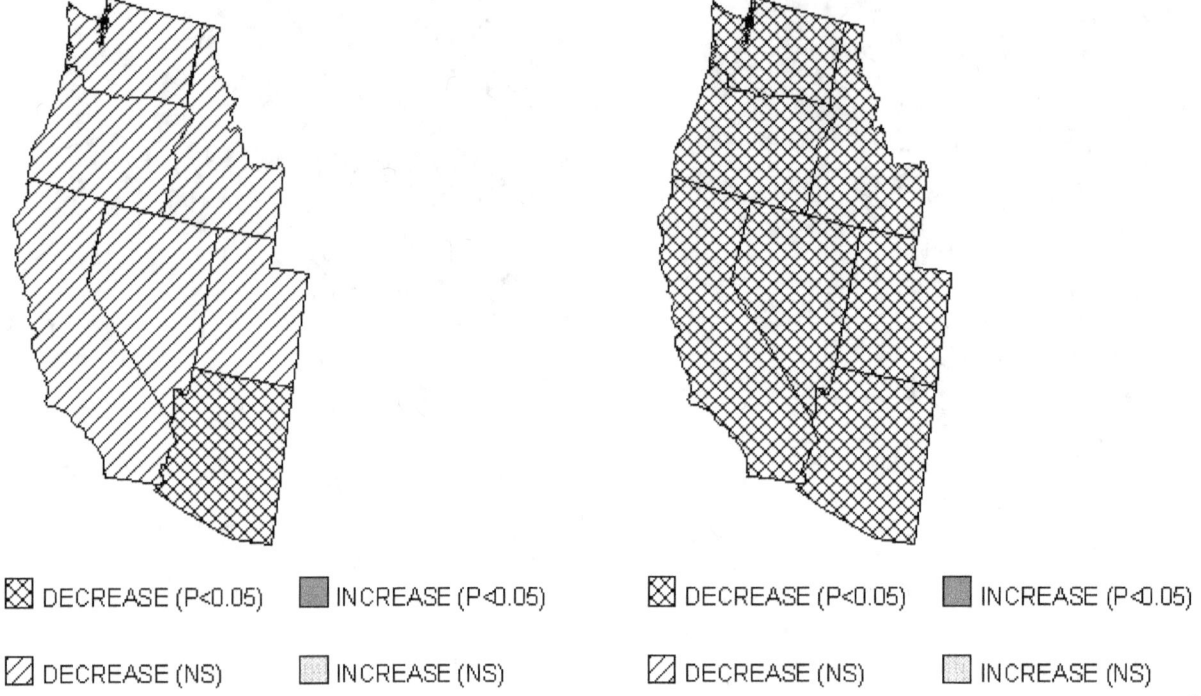

Fig. 13. Trends in number of mourning doves heard per route by state in the Western Management Unit, 1992-2001.

Population Trends: 10 and 36-year.--A significant decline in numbers of doves heard was indicated for both time periods (Table 1). Analyses of doves seen also indicated significant declines over both time periods.

Trends by state are illustrated in Figs. 13 and 14, and Table 1. Arizona shows a decline over 10 years while all states in the Unit have a decline between 1966 and 2001.

BREEDING BIRD SURVEY RESULTS

There has been considerable discussion about utilizing the North American Breeding Bird Survey (BBS) as a measure of mourning dove abundance. Consequently, we are including trend information in this report to enable readers to compare BBS results with the Mourning Dove Call-count Survey (CCS) results from last year's mourning dove status report (Dolton and Smith 2000). Sauer et al. (1994) discussed the differences in the methodology of the 2 surveys. The BBS is based on 50-stop routes that are surveyed in

Fig. 14. Trends in number of mourning doves heard per route by state in the Western Management Unit, 1966-2001.

June. Also, with the BBS, data for doves heard and seen are combined for analyses while those data are analyzed separately with the CCS. Unfortunately, BBS data are not available in time for use in regulations development during the year of the survey. Trends calculated from BBS data for the 10-year period (1991-2000) and over 35 years (1966-2000) are presented in Table 3.

In general, trends indicated by the BBS tend to indicate fewer declines. The major differences occur in the Eastern Unit. This is likely due to the larger sample size of BBS survey routes and greater consistency of coverage by BBS routes in the Unit (Sauer et al. 1994), although additional analyses are needed to clarify some differences in results between surveys within states.

For the 10-year period, the CCS indicated a significant decline (*P*<0.05) in doves heard for the combined hunting states in the EMU while the BBS showed no trend (*P*=0.6458). For the nonhunting states, the CCS showed no trend (*P*>0.10) while the BBS showed a significant increase (*P*<0.01). For the EMU as a whole, there was a significant decline ($P<0.05$) with the CCS while the BBS showed no trend ($P=0.5424$). For the CMU, the CCS showed a significant decline ($P<0.05$) while the BBS showed no trend ($P=0.1783$). In the WMU, the CCS indicated a significant decline ($P<0.01$) while the BBS showed no trend ($P=0.1002$).

Over 35 years, results were very similar with both surveys for the Central and Western Management Units with both surveys indicating significant declines (BBS: $P<0.01$ for both Units; CCS: $P<0.05$ for CMU, $P<0.01$ for WMU). In the Eastern Unit, CCS analyses indicated a tendency toward a decline ($P<0.10$) over the period. In contrast, the BBS showed an increase ($P<0.01$). The combined hunting states in the EMU showed a decline ($P<0.01$) with the CCS, while there was no trend indicated with the BBS ($P=0.6544$). The nonhunting states of the EMU were different also. The CCS showed no trend ($P>0.10$), but BBS data indicated a significant increase ($P<0.01$).

HARVEST ESTIMATES

State Surveys

In past years, a compilation of nonuniform, periodic state harvest surveys has been used to obtain rough estimates of the number of mourning doves killed and the number of dove hunters. These figures have been summarized by Sadler (1993). In general, mourning dove harvest in the EMU was relatively constant from 1966-87, with between 27.5 and 28.5 million birds taken. The latest estimate, a 1989 survey, indicated harvest had dropped to about 26.4 million birds shot by an estimated 1.3 million hunters. In the CMU, although hunting pressure and harvest varied widely among states, dove harvest in the Unit generally increased between 1966-87 to an annual average of about 13.5 million birds. In 1989, almost 11 million doves were taken by about 747,000 hunters. Dove harvest in the WMU has declined significantly over the years following a decline in the breeding population. In the early 1970's, about 7.3 million doves were taken by an estimated 450,000 hunters. By 1989, the harvest had dropped to about 4 million birds shot by approximately 285,000 hunters.

In summary, it appears that the dove harvest throughout the United States is on the decrease. However, the mourning dove remains an extremely important game bird, as more doves are harvested than all other migratory game birds combined. A 1991 survey indicated that doves provided about 9.5 million days of hunting recreation for 1.9 million people (U.S. Department of the Interior, Fish and Wildlife Service and U.S. Department of Commerce, Bureau of the Census 1993). A survey conducted in 1996 estimated that doves were hunted about 8.1 million days by 1.6 million people (U.S. Department of the Interior, Fish and Wildlife Service and U.S. Department of Commerce, Bureau of the Census 1997).

Harvest Information Program (HIP)

Wildlife professionals have long recognized that reliable harvest estimates are needed to monitor the impact of hunting. States have established harvest surveys to meet their individual needs for game species, and a federal waterfowl harvest survey has been conducted since 1952. However, there are serious problems with using either current state or federal harvest surveys to monitor the national or regional harvests of mourning doves and other non-waterfowl migratory game birds, especially on an annual basis. The federal waterfowl hunter survey system of obtaining names and addresses of duck stamp buyers is inadequate because non-waterfowl hunters are excluded. More than half the nation's migratory game bird hunters do not hunt waterfowl, thus, they cannot be sampled by that survey. Attempts to use state harvest surveys to obtain coordinated national and regional estimates have been unsuccessful because sample frames and survey methodologies vary widely among states.

To remedy these problems, state wildlife agencies and the U.S. Fish and Wildlife Service initiated the national, cooperative Harvest Information Program in 1992. This program is designed to enable the Service to conduct harvest surveys that will provide reliable annual estimates of the harvest of mourning doves and other migratory upland game bird species. Under the Harvest Information Program, states provide the Service with the names and addresses of all licensed migratory bird hunters each year, and the Service conducts surveys to estimate the harvest in each state.

California, Missouri, and South Dakota voluntarily participated in a 2-year pilot stage of the Harvest Information Program in 1992 and 1993, and each year since then more states have entered the program. In

1998, all states except Hawaii participated in the program.

Results of mourning dove harvest surveys conducted for the 1999-00 hunting season are presented in Table 4 and preliminary results from the 2000-01 season are shown in Table 5. Total estimated harvest for the 2000-01 season by management unit and for the U.S. are as follows: Eastern: 10,292,200 ••8%; Central: 13,102,800 ••6%; Western: 2,024,500 ••9%; and, U.S.: 25,419,500 ••5%. It is important to note that these estimates do not necessary indicate that the harvest has declined. They cannot be compared directly with earlier estimates since they are based on a different sampling scheme. The reliability of these estimates depends primarily upon the quality of the sample frame provided by each participating state. If a state's sample frame does not include all migratory bird hunters in that state, the survey results underestimate hunter activity and harvest for the state.

The Harvest Surveys Section is continuing to work with states to improve the accuracy and precision of the harvest estimates.. In the future, results will be presented by state within dove management unit.

ACKNOWLEDGMENTS

Personnel of state wildlife agencies and the U.S. Fish and Wildlife Service (USFWS) cooperated in collecting the data presented in this report. T. Nguyen (USFWS) assisted R. D. Holmes (USFWS) with database development and a new Internet web site that allows cooperators to submit survey data electronically. K.A. Wilkins, P.R. Garrettson, R.V. Raftovich, and J. P. Bladen (USFWS) provided invaluable assistance with data entry. F. Fiehrer and L. Whitman (USGS-BRD) helped with creation of the database and printing of survey forms. W. L. Kendall (BRD) and J. R. Sauer (BRD) analyzed the data and provided statistical support. P. I. Padding (USFWS) provided the HIP data and explanation. P. D. Keywood (USFWS) assisted with graphics preparation.

LITERATURE CITED

Aldrich, J.W. 1993. Classification and distribution. Pages 47-54 in T.S. Baskett, M.W. Sayre, R.E. Tomlinson, and R.E. Mirarchi, eds., Ecology and management of the mourning dove. Stackpole Books, Harrisburg, PA.

Dolton, D.D. 1993. The call-count survey: historic development and current procedures. Pages 233-252 in T.S. Baskett, M.W. Sayre, R.E. Tomlinson, and R.E. Mirarchi, eds., Ecology and management of the mourning dove. Stackpole Books, Harrisburg, PA.

Dolton, D.D. and G.W. Smith. 2000. Mouring dove breeding population status, 2000. U.S. Fish and Wildlife Service, Laurel, Maryland. 29pp

Dunks, J.H., R.E. Tomlinson, H.M. Reeves, D.D. Dolton, C.E. Braun and T.P. Zapatka. 1982. Mourning dove banding analysis, Central Management Unit, 1967-77. Special Scientific Report--Wildl. No. 249. U.S. Fish and Wildlife Service, Washington, DC. 128 pp.

Foote, L.E. and H.S. Peters. 1952. Pages 1-2 in Investigations of methods of appraising the abundance of mourning doves. U.S. Fish and Wildlife Service, Special Scientific Report--Wildlife 17.

Geissler, P.H. and J.R. Sauer. 1990. Topics in route regression analysis. Pages 54-57 in J.R. Sauer and S. Droege, eds. Survey designs and statistical methods for the estimation of avian population trends. U.S. Fish and Wildlife Service, Biological Reptort 90(1).

Kiel, W.H. 1959. Mourning dove management units, a progress report. U.S. Fish and Wildlife Service, Special Scientific Report--Wildlife 42.

____. 1961. The mourning dove program for the future. Transactions of the North American Wildlife and Natural Resources Conference 26:418-435.

Link, W.A. and J.R. Sauer. 1994. Estimating equations estimates of trends. Bird Populations 2:23-32.

McClure, H.E. 1939. Cooing activity and censusing of the mourning dove. Journal of Wildlife Management 3:323-328.

Mirarchi, R.E. and T.S. Baskett. 1994. Mourning dove (*Zenaida macroura*). *In* A. Poole and F. Gill, eds., The birds of North America, No. 117. The Academy of Natural Sciences, Philadelphia and The American Ornithologists' Union, Washington, D.C. 32 pp.

Peterjohn, B.G., J.R. Sauer and W.A. Link. 1994. The 1992 and 1993 summary of the North American breeding bird survey. Bird Populations 2:46-61.

Sadler, K.C. 1993. Mourning dove harvest. Pages 449-458 *in* T.S.Baskett, M.W. Sayer, R.E. Tomlinson and R.E. Mirarchi, eds., Ecology and management of the mourning dove. Stackpole Books, Harrisburg, PA.

Sauer, J.R. and P.H. Geissler. 1990. Annual indices from route regression analyses. Pages 58-62 *in* J.R. Sauer and S. Droege, eds. Survey designs and statistical methods for the estimation of avian population trends. U.S. Fish and Wildlife Service, Biological Report. 90(1).

Sauer, J.R., D.D. Dolton, and S. Droege. 1994.Mourning dove population trend estimates from Call-count and North American Breeding Bird Surveys. Journal of Wildlife Management. 58(3):506-515.

Tomlinson, R.E., D.D. Dolton, H.M. Reeves, J.D. Nichols and L.A. McKibben. 1988. Migration, harvest, and population characteristics of mourning doves banded in the Western Management Unit; 1964-1977. Fish and Wildlife Technical. Report 13, U.S. Fish and Wildlife Service, Washington, DC. 101pp.

U. S. Department of the Interior, Fish and Wildlife Service and U.S. Department of Commerce, Bureau of the Census. 1993. 1991 National survey of fishing, hunting, and wildlife-associated recreation. U.S. Government Printing Office, Washington, DC. 124 pp.

U. S. Department of the Interior, Fish and Wildlife Service and U.S. Department of Commerce, Bureau of the Census. 1997. 1996 National survey of fishing, hunting, and wildlife-associated recreation. U.S. Government Printing Office, Washington, DC. 115 pp.

Table 1.Trends (% change[a] per year as determined by linear regression) in number of mourning doves heard along call-count survey routes, 1966-2001.

	2 year (2000-2001)					10 year (1992-2001)					36 year (1966-2001)				
	N	% Change		90% CI		N	% Change		90% CI		N	% Change		90% CI	
EASTERN UNIT															
Hunt															
AL	23	-1.5		-18.7	15.7	28	-1.7	*	-3.2	-0.3	42	-0.6		-1.4	0.2
DE/MD	9	22.4	**	5.7	39.1	14	-0.1		-2.7	2.6	19	-1.6	**	-2.9	-0.3
FL	14	-12.6		-36.5	11.3	23	-1.4		-3.3	0.4	28	0.3		-0.6	1.2
GA	17	27.6	*	3.1	52.2	21	-3.8	***	-6.1	-1.4	28	-0.9	**	-1.5	-0.3
IL	12	-10.5		-23.0	2.0	20	-0.5		-3.7	2.8	22	0.7		-0.6	1.9
IN	8	-5.1		-26.4	16.2	15	-3.5	***	-5.0	-2.0	18	-1.5	**	-2.6	-0.5
KY	15	-3.1		-24.5	18.4	20	1.2		-0.8	3.2	25	-0.5		-1.8	0.8
LA	12	9.5		-17.1	36.1	19	1.0		-1.6	3.6	23	1.2	*	0.1	2.2
MS	16	-9.0		-24.4	6.3	23	-2.4		-5.0	0.2	31	-1.7	*	-3.4	-0.0
NC	16	12.3		-2.1	26.8	21	1.7	**	0.4	3.1	24	0.0		-1.1	1.1
OH[c]	35	-11.3		-22.8	0.1	37	-1.7		-3.9	0.6	57	-1.1	***	-1.7	-0.5
PA	10	-10.6		-24.6	3.4	17	1.0		-2.2	4.1	17	1.1		-0.8	2.9
SC	15	7.2		-7.7	22.2	20	-1.3		-3.3	0.8	25	-1.2	*	-2.2	-0.1
TN	17	-11.5	**	-21.0	-2.1	25	-2.7	*	-5.2	-0.1	32	-1.6	**	-2.6	-0.6
VA	24	-2.6		-15.2	10.0	33	0.9		-1.5	3.3	33	-2.5	*	-4.6	-0.3
WV	7	54.9	*	0.0	109.7	10	-1.1		-3.3	1.2	11	1.7		-0.4	3.7
Subunit	250	-3.6		-8.8	1.6	346	-1.2	***	-1.9	-0.6	435	-0.6	***	-1.0	-0.2
Nonhunt															
MI	11	-22.9	***	-34.7	-11.1	21	-0.1		-2.5	2.4	22	0.0		-1.5	1.6
N.England[d]	30	-8.9		-22.3	4.5	43	-1.8		-3.7	0.0	76	1.9	***	0.8	2.9
NJ	7	-30.7	***	-43.7	-17.8	11	-0.1		-7.8	7.6	20	-1.8		-4.8	1.2
NY	11	-23.8		-63.4	15.8	17	3.0	**	0.7	5.2	20	1.5		-0.8	3.8
WI	15	-2.8		-19.1	13.5	22	-0.5		-3.2	2.2	23	0.3		-0.8	1.5
Subunit	74	-16.2	***	-24.6	-7.9	114	-0.3		-1.6	1.1	161	0.5		-0.3	1.2
Unit	324	-6.1	**	-10.6	-1.6	460	-1.0	***	-1.6	-0.4	596	-0.4	*	-0.8	-0.1
CENTRAL UNIT															
AR	10	3.3		-14.8	21.4	15	-1.2		-3.5	1.1	16	-0.7		-1.8	0.4
CO	6	-31.2	***	-45.7	-16.8	17	2.7		-1.8	7.2	21	1.7		-0.4	3.8
IA	12	-5.8		-26.0	14.5	16	-2.0		-5.3	1.3	17	0.2		-0.7	1.1
KS	15	-24.2	**	-43.0	-5.3	28	1.7		-2.1	5.4	33	0.1		-0.6	0.8
MN	6	-26.1	***	-30.3	-22.0	12	-3.6	*	-6.9	-0.3	13	-1.2		-3.0	0.6
MO	16	-2.7		-25.6	20.2	21	-4.3	**	-7.0	-1.5	28	-2.2	***	-3.5	-0.9
MT	6	-24.6	***	-35.0	-14.2	20	6.1	***	2.7	9.6	27	-1.8		-3.8	0.2
NE	18	-10.3		-21.0	0.4	24	-1.7		-3.6	0.2	27	-0.8	*	-1.5	-0.1
NM	6	13.1	***	8.6	17.7	28	2.3		-1.3	6.0	31	0.8		-0.5	2.1
ND	21	-13.1	*	-25.5	-0.8	27	-2.6	*	-5.1	-0.1	30	0.5		-1.0	1.9
OK	12	-11.0		-34.9	13.0	17	0.7		-3.5	4.8	25	-0.9		-3.5	1.8
SD	14	-11.0		-26.8	4.7	21	-1.1		-3.7	1.5	28	-0.8		-2.2	0.6
TX	104	-4.9		-13.7	3.9	139	-1.8	**	-3.0	-0.6	198	-0.4		-1.1	0.3
WY	8	-30.2	***	-48.6	-11.7	16	-3.1		-7.4	1.3	21	-3.2	*	-6.0	-0.5
Unit	254	-9.4	***	-14.6	-4.2	401	-1.3	***	-2.0	-0.6	515	-0.5	**	-0.9	-0.2
WESTERN UNIT															
AZ	17	33.2	**	10.3	56.1	56	-2.8	**	-5.0	-0.7	69	-1.1	**	-1.9	-0.3
CA	40	-18.2	**	-32.0	-4.4	60	-1.6	*	-3.0	-0.2	80	-2.6	***	-3.7	-1.5
ID	7	-47.7	**	-79.3	-16.1	22	-2.6		-8.1	3.0	26	-3.1	**	-5.4	-0.9
NV	8	-35.8	***	-52.4	-19.1	26	-4.3		-9.6	1.1	31	-5.9	***	-7.8	-4.1
OR	7	44.9		-6.1	95.9	19	-0.5		-2.8	1.8	25	-3.1	**	-5.2	-1.0
UT	5	-56.3	***	-78.4	-34.2	17	-1.6		-6.1	2.9	19	-3.8	**	-6.9	-0.6
WA	15	13.0		-14.6	40.6	21	-2.7		-7.8	2.3	26	-2.5	**	-4.5	-0.4
Unit	99	-7.1		-15.6	1.4	221	-2.5	***	-3.8	-1.2	276	-2.2	***	-2.9	-1.6

[a] Mean of route trends weighted by land area and population density. The estimated count in the next year is (%/100+1) times the count in the current year where % is the annual change. Note: Extrapolating the estimated trend statistic (% change per year) over time (e.g., 36 years) may exaggerate the total change over the period.
[b] *$P<0.1$; **$P<0.05$; ***$P<0.01$.
[c] Ohio became a hunting state in 1995.
[d] New England consists of CT, ME, MA, NH, RI, and VT.

Table 2. Breeding population indices[a] based on mourning doves heard along Call-count routes, 1966-2001.

Management unit/state	year								
	1966	1967	1968	1969	1970	1971	1972	1973	1974
EASTERN UNIT									
Hunt									
AL	26.3	23.5	21.2	21.5	21.8	17.9	25.6	22.4	17.0
DE/MD	16.5	20.2	14.1	15.0	18.5	15.7	17.2	17.0	18.0
FL	11.4	10.8	9.3	9.9	12.6	10.6	10.9	11.1	13.4
GA	29.4	27.9	24.0	25.7	32.5	25.6	24.4	26.9	27.9
IL	22.0	19.0	22.6	19.6	22.8	20.9	21.5	21.2	17.9
IN	37.5	34.5	33.9	32.8	31.7	42.8	37.4	33.4	31.9
KY	24.0	21.7	21.2	22.2	26.7	23.9	20.1	23.8	27.6
LA	10.5	10.7	10.0	11.7	7.9	10.5	11.6	9.0	10.5
MS	39.8	34.2	29.0	26.9	29.7	30.2	33.7	30.2	24.3
NC	34.5	27.9	29.5	42.0	48.5	28.2	22.9	43.6	24.9
OH[c]	24.1	22.7	20.5	23.4	23.1	23.9	24.9	19.8	24.1
PA	8.7	9.3	8.6	8.3	5.4	6.3	8.8	5.7	8.5
SC	31.3	34.2	34.9	33.6	31.6	27.7	24.6	28.1	26.1
TN	32.0	23.4	24.0	23.8	32.3	22.8	28.8	21.9	23.4
VA	27.9	22.8	26.1	23.0	29.5	23.6	14.2	16.6	22.5
WV	6.3	5.3	5.4	5.9	5.5	5.0	6.6	3.9	4.1
Subunit	23.6	21.6	20.6	21.2	22.1	20.2	20.8	19.7	20.0
Nonhunt									
MI	14.5	15.6	10.3	10.5	8.5	16.8	17.3	13.6	11.5
N.England[b]	5.7	6.1	5.6	4.8	5.7	6.0	6.7	7.9	5.0
NJ	19.0	16.2	20.1	18.5	25.0	23.7	24.9	22.0	21.5
NY	6.7	6.8	6.4	6.3	7.7	9.0	7.1	7.4	7.6
WI	10.6	13.7	13.7	10.5	11.3	16.4	17.1	11.2	11.9
Subunit	10.0	11.1	9.6	8.7	9.0	12.7	12.8	10.8	9.7
Unit	19.9	19.0	17.7	17.7	18.4	18.6	19.1	17.5	17.3
CENTRAL UNIT									
AR	21.5	22.4	21.5	20.7	22.4	22.5	21.1	23.7	22.0
CO	16.4	17.0	15.7	21.6	22.1	16.1	21.6	14.1	22.7
IA	30.1	27.0	29.1	26.4	19.1	23.5	31.4	29.7	23.2
KS	46.5	46.9	48.6	49.3	45.4	46.3	51.7	46.1	45.8
MN	29.3	23.6	25.4	18.8	15.1	21.7	25.0	19.0	26.1
MO	40.3	38.0	47.6	28.7	39.6	33.2	44.9	33.7	28.8
MT	27.6	25.5	20.0	22.1	17.7	25.1	20.0	14.4	16.7
NE	44.7	39.2	50.1	49.0	47.5	45.1	43.6	41.8	43.2
NM	14.8	11.0	15.4	11.8	11.5	10.9	12.5	8.9	10.9
ND	36.5	35.3	48.2	40.1	35.7	37.0	38.3	42.6	41.8
OK	24.0	29.7	34.8	33.6	26.3	18.9	30.3	28.4	29.5
SD	54.1	33.9	46.3	39.3	46.7	41.0	40.8	42.9	51.3
TX	26.3	21.8	21.5	19.5	20.6	20.0	26.7	21.4	22.8
WY	22.8	24.0	12.5	20.2	19.2	10.8	14.6	14.5	20.8
Unit	29.6	26.5	27.3	26.1	25.2	24.8	28.3	23.6	26.5
WESTERN UNIT									
AZ	29.2	29.4	26.5	31.2	31.2	21.1	23.7	28.6	24.7
CA	28.2	26.7	24.6	24.2	23.6	17.7	21.5	20.6	22.3
ID	18.9	19.4	17.3	18.0	16.8	13.1	12.5	15.2	12.6
NV	13.7	12.2	28.8	19.0	13.8	8.2	10.9	7.5	10.1
OR	16.9	11.2	13.3	12.0	9.1	7.9	7.8	7.6	13.3
UT	21.5	32.9	16.6	15.7	18.3	25.6	14.9	12.9	14.7
WA	11.0	16.2	15.1	12.0	12.2	14.4	10.3	9.4	11.8
Unit	19.5	19.7	20.3	19.2	17.7	14.6	14.7	14.3	16.2

[a]Annual indices are the predicted value from the trend analysis plus the deviation from the expected value in a year. Large but nonsignificant changes due to small sample sizes produce exaggerated indices over the 36-year period.
[b] New England consists of CT, ME, MA, NH, RI, and VT.
[c] Ohio became a hunting state in 1995.

13

Table 2. Breeding population indices[a] based on mourning doves heard along Call-count routes, 1966-2001.

Management unit/state	year								
	1975	1976	1977	1978	1979	1980	1981	1982	1983
EASTERN UNIT									
Hunt									
AL	21.7	20.8	23.0	25.3	24.3	24.3	23.3	23.7	23.8
DE/MD	12.8	15.6	14.4	15.1	14.7	13.9	13.3	13.9	9.9
FL	14.0	12.9	14.2	11.1	12.1	9.7	8.9	10.5	12.2
GA	30.3	23.8	24.8	26.9	23.5	24.1	26.6	28.6	25.5
IL	25.2	24.8	26.6	20.5	17.9	18.3	20.7	25.2	26.0
IN	33.6	33.8	37.6	20.4	21.6	27.4	31.5	22.3	19.2
KY	19.5	24.4	22.9	24.4	16.8	16.3	27.7	23.9	13.2
LA	11.0	11.1	9.1	10.7	9.1	12.7	11.0	13.8	13.0
MS	25.8	26.3	27.1	30.6	26.2	24.7	24.7	31.0	26.0
NC	14.0	17.0	45.5	24.3	28.8	27.9	27.5	23.0	27.2
OH[c]	36.8	26.9	25.7	13.6	13.2	15.9	19.4	18.5	19.5
PA	5.9	6.0	4.9	6.0	6.8	8.0	9.4	9.0	9.0
SC	25.9	25.6	21.8	28.8	24.4	30.7	29.8	30.8	29.3
TN	22.4	22.1	24.2	29.9	20.5	22.2	18.7	25.0	19.3
VA	25.1	23.8	31.7	23.4	20.7	20.1	17.3	19.0	18.7
WV	2.4	6.0	5.7	6.5	7.3	8.4	6.8	6.5	6.2
Subunit	19.9	20.0	21.2	19.5	18.0	19.1	19.5	20.6	19.2
Nonhunt									
MI	12.9	13.1	10.9	12.5	7.3	13.4	15.3	11.1	9.9
N.England[b]	4.8	4.5	8.5	7.3	6.1	7.6	9.2	7.5	8.0
NJ	15.5	19.4	21.3	16.9	18.0	16.7	14.0	16.0	19.0
NY	13.3	7.8	7.8	9.4	6.3	11.1	9.5	10.1	9.4
WI	14.9	14.9	19.6	7.9	11.5	14.8	20.0	11.0	13.0
Subunit	11.9	10.5	12.0	9.7	8.2	12.2	13.8	10.5	10.6
Unit	18.0	17.7	19.0	16.9	15.2	17.5	18.4	17.9	17.0
CENTRAL UNIT									
AR	21.1	25.7	21.0	14.8	12.1	20.0	21.9	25.5	19.2
CO	17.0	24.1	23.1	26.1	22.6	27.2	31.6	30.7	17.3
IA	21.6	26.8	20.8	23.4	20.0	27.0	29.8	21.5	15.4
KS	44.0	48.4	46.0	35.8	52.8	57.3	54.9	52.3	59.0
MN	28.4	25.0	29.1	28.0	28.5	30.9	27.4	24.0	21.3
MO	33.7	29.8	34.5	22.1	21.0	32.6	27.5	24.2	23.4
MT	22.8	16.5	20.2	19.4	19.3	17.7	16.5	21.1	17.0
NE	40.7	45.8	46.5	38.4	41.3	52.6	50.0	49.0	44.6
NM	13.6	13.3	11.9	12.0	8.1	13.2	13.1	10.2	13.9
ND	30.7	49.5	41.0	44.1	41.4	47.0	47.4	44.5	42.9
OK	26.6	28.2	35.6	27.2	26.2	26.9	26.6	27.7	28.5
SD	43.4	46.5	40.6	43.7	42.7	42.8	38.4	45.7	39.4
TX	20.6	20.2	19.2	20.1	24.9	23.7	21.6	20.9	19.4
WY	18.3	16.9	10.7	16.9	12.8	11.6	12.7	16.3	10.9
Unit	26.0	26.7	25.6	25.2	24.8	27.8	27.0	27.0	24.0
WESTERN UNIT									
AZ	27.1	28.0	25.1	25.2	24.6	21.9	24.7	28.3	22.0
CA	18.8	22.5	17.2	15.5	11.9	20.2	16.7	20.7	12.8
ID	8.7	16.0	19.6	10.7	10.3	10.7	11.7	12.1	9.2
NV	6.0	9.7	9.9	5.9	8.4	11.7	8.4	4.5	4.0
OR	9.8	10.3	11.5	6.0	6.2	9.2	7.8	7.6	5.8
UT	15.7	18.2	21.4	9.4	11.7	14.1	18.6	11.2	11.2
WA	12.7	12.3	13.3	8.6	12.1	8.2	9.9	9.2	7.8
Unit	14.0	17.5	17.3	11.7	12.4	15.3	14.9	13.7	10.7

[a] Annual indices are the predicted value from the trend analysis plus the deviation from the expected value in a year.
Large but nonsignificant changes due to small sample sizes produce exaggerated indices over the 36-year period.
[b] New England consists of CT, ME, MA, NH, RI, and VT.
[c] Ohio became a hunting state in 1995.

14

Table 2. Breeding population indices[a] based on mourning doves heard along Call-count routes, 1966-2001.

Management unit/state	year								
	1984	1985	1986	1987	1988	1989	1990	1991	1992
EASTERN UNIT									
Hunt									
AL	19.9	25.4	23.1	20.6	22.7	19.4	18.2	17.0	19.6
DE/MD	11.3	12.3	14.7	12.8	11.8	16.3	7.8	12.1	15.5
FL	8.4	10.8	12.6	11.4	13.8	12.6	11.3	12.2	12.5
GA	20.6	26.6	24.1	24.8	25.0	25.4	26.1	21.5	30.2
IL	21.1	18.3	25.3	24.9	28.2	27.8	27.1	27.5	28.6
IN	20.9	18.3	24.4	24.5	29.5	25.0	27.2	27.4	24.2
KY	21.2	22.1	19.8	24.4	19.4	26.6	22.1	21.1	16.8
LA	11.9	10.6	9.8	14.1	10.5	16.5	11.8	12.0	16.0
MS	19.3	25.6	25.1	22.3	26.4	24.7	20.9	17.3	22.5
NC	30.5	21.2	29.7	28.8	26.5	31.3	28.8	24.5	23.7
OH[c]	18.1	17.0	16.5	18.0	20.6	19.3	17.7	19.0	19.9
PA	8.2	9.0	9.6	10.9	7.4	9.5	9.5	9.7	10.9
SC	26.6	26.7	22.6	33.1	26.2	25.1	27.1	22.0	21.6
TN	16.5	21.3	16.2	19.9	19.5	17.8	15.6	18.7	18.3
VA	18.2	16.7	13.6	14.0	15.2	14.9	12.6	13.3	11.6
WV	5.5	6.8	6.5	6.8	7.9	8.4	11.1	9.3	7.5
Subunit	17.4	18.5	18.6	19.7	19.6	20.3	18.7	18.2	19.3
Nonhunt									
MI	10.5	11.5	14.7	12.0	14.5	18.0	13.5	11.1	12.8
N.England[b]	7.0	7.7	8.4	8.0	7.5	7.9	8.9	9.7	10.4
NJ	12.0	12.4	14.6	13.4	13.0	15.9	12.8	15.4	10.0
NY	9.1	8.4	7.0	9.2	7.5	11.5	10.1	12.6	10.7
WI	10.1	10.4	11.3	7.4	17.5	17.5	14.0	12.8	19.5
Subunit	9.5	9.9	10.6	9.3	11.6	13.8	11.8	11.7	13.2
Unit	15.3	16.2	16.5	16.8	17.6	18.9	17.1	16.7	17.9
CENTRAL UNIT									
AR	13.7	13.6	14.7	13.8	15.3	21.5	16.7	15.1	18.2
CO	22.4	27.4	26.6	29.2	32.9	37.4	34.0	22.7	17.4
IA	22.6	25.0	22.6	21.7	29.3	27.5	31.7	23.4	31.4
KS	46.7	60.3	41.6	45.2	52.2	45.8	39.8	57.2	55.6
MN	18.1	19.8	18.2	23.4	23.8	19.0	15.6	19.4	22.6
MO	22.2	21.2	22.0	24.8	24.9	24.4	19.8	21.4	22.0
MT	12.8	17.7	18.5	17.7	14.6	18.6	20.3	13.4	14.3
NE	42.6	43.8	35.9	36.1	36.1	40.2	40.0	40.8	38.3
NM	14.9	12.8	15.3	18.5	13.9	15.5	17.0	15.7	10.3
ND	33.7	44.2	41.2	47.5	44.9	47.1	46.1	51.0	54.8
OK	21.2	20.6	22.8	24.9	22.0	16.3	21.4	21.4	23.1
SD	43.6	40.9	37.9	33.2	39.3	42.2	43.7	45.8	37.2
TX	19.0	19.7	21.3	20.9	21.5	16.4	17.5	24.3	22.2
WY	9.8	11.3	13.8	11.1	7.2	8.5	8.5	9.0	9.3
Unit	22.5	24.5	24.8	25.5	24.5	24.3	24.4	24.9	23.9
WESTERN UNIT									
AZ	27.0	21.8	25.8	17.4	19.5	23.7	18.4	23.1	24.8
CA	17.8	12.6	14.5	11.2	14.9	11.0	11.0	10.8	11.7
ID	10.7	9.8	6.9	7.0	9.1	9.0	9.7	8.9	8.2
NV	4.0	5.0	3.3	3.8	5.1	4.4	3.1	4.0	3.4
OR	7.2	7.9	6.3	5.7	7.1	5.8	6.5	4.1	6.3
UT	12.7	8.4	11.6	10.1	10.4	10.9	9.3	8.4	10.8
WA	6.8	8.5	10.2	8.1	8.1	7.1	7.3	9.2	8.1
Unit	12.6	11.4	11.2	9.7	11.8	10.8	9.9	10.1	10.7

[a] Annual indices are the predicted value from the trend analysis plus the deviation from the expected value in a year.
Large but nonsignificant changes due to small sample sizes produce exaggerated indices over the 36-year period.
[b] New England consists of CT, ME, MA, NH, RI, and VT.
[c] Ohio became a hunting state in 1995.

15

Table 2. Breeding population indices[a] based on mourning doves heard along Call-count routes, 1966-2001.

Management unit/state	year								
	1993	1994	1995	1996	1997	1998	1999	2000	2001
EASTERN UNIT									
Hunt									
AL	21.3	22.2	23.5	18.2	17.1	18.9	18.2	19.4	18.1
DE/MD	10.6	12.8	11.5	10.8	8.9	12.3	8.9	8.7	7.8
FL	11.1	10.6	12.2	11.4	10.4	13.0	13.9	13.4	10.6
GA	18.8	21.4	25.6	21.5	18.6	17.9	18.0	16.4	22.7
IL	25.2	28.2	29.2	23.0	23.5	23.6	21.8	28.4	24.0
IN	25.6	30.4	24.7	21.2	21.0	21.2	22.1	23.8	20.2
KY	21.6	20.8	20.4	17.9	16.9	21.8	21.9	23.3	18.7
LA	12.2	13.3	14.9	12.1	12.5	14.2	14.9	17.0	16.9
MS	24.7	20.8	19.0	17.8	16.8	17.0	20.5	17.9	16.2
NC	24.6	24.9	27.1	27.5	30.3	29.7	30.3	35.9	39.9
OH[c]	16.8	18.7	17.1	14.1	14.1	16.6	17.1	18.4	15.1
PA	12.0	11.4	11.0	10.6	9.7	11.8	9.8	11.4	10.7
SC	25.5	22.9	18.2	22.7	21.7	24.5	22.3	21.3	22.2
TN	16.1	19.8	18.2	15.5	16.6	16.2	16.4	18.3	14.6
VA	13.1	12.8	13.6	10.9	13.8	12.9	12.8	13.7	12.1
WV	8.7	9.5	9.8	4.9	10.3	8.6	10.0	9.6	6.5
Subunit	18.4	19.0	19.2	16.5	16.7	17.9	17.9	18.9	17.2
Nonhunt									
MI	11.8	11.2	12.5	12.8	12.3	14.0	13.6	17.7	13.6
N.England[b]	10.8	9.8	12.4	8.6	8.7	9.4	10.9	11.4	9.6
NJ	16.1	14.0	10.3	13.3	7.2	11.8	9.5	13.9	7.2
NY	9.5	9.7	10.6	9.9	10.7	9.3	12.3	13.6	11.7
WI	18.1	15.3	12.8	11.6	12.1	9.7	18.2	16.5	16.6
Subunit	12.6	11.6	12.0	10.8	10.8	10.7	13.6	14.9	12.6
Unit	17.1	17.2	17.5	15.2	15.3	16.1	17.1	18.1	16.3
CENTRAL UNIT									
AR	16.5	19.8	18.4	18.6	20.1	19.6	17.9	17.4	18.3
CO	17.0	29.8	25.6	19.4	26.6	29.8	37.0	33.3	27.6
IA	23.5	24.8	26.4	33.7	27.7	28.9	27.9	24.5	28.1
KS	37.0	50.9	58.9	32.8	59.6	54.1	65.9	50.9	41.3
MN	16.4	20.0	19.4	18.6	19.7	18.4	16.5	17.0	12.9
MO	21.4	25.7	22.3	21.8	21.3	19.0	17.5	18.3	15.5
MT	10.3	9.7	12.3	12.3	11.5	14.4	13.1	13.8	11.8
NE	40.3	37.4	40.9	34.3	31.9	40.4	36.7	37.2	31.6
NM	11.5	14.5	13.0	11.3	15.0	12.6	14.7	16.9	15.5
ND	47.5	41.2	43.6	45.1	40.3	35.9	48.5	47.9	46.0
OK	19.8	25.5	19.3	20.3	19.5	28.0	25.2	21.1	20.5
SD	33.4	36.4	38.6	37.9	32.5	35.3	36.5	37.7	33.7
TX	20.2	22.4	16.8	14.5	21.5	21.7	21.4	18.8	19.2
WY	6.8	8.6	6.3	7.3	7.1	7.6	5.7	8.1	4.7
Unit	20.7	24.1	22.4	20.6	23.3	24.2	24.3	23.8	21.2
WESTERN UNIT									
AZ	25.1	22.2	21.2	12.4	19.1	22.0	23.3	22.4	22.2
CA	14.2	11.9	11.8	11.7	10.3	10.4	11.0	10.2	9.9
ID	6.8	6.9	6.3	6.0	8.5	5.0	7.0	6.9	4.7
NV	2.7	2.4	4.0	3.6	3.2	2.8	3.3	2.7	2.4
OR	5.2	6.1	5.1	4.9	4.9	3.7	3.8	6.2	4.2
UT	9.0	9.3	6.1	7.1	8.9	5.2	8.2	13.5	6.2
WA	7.0	7.3	8.1	5.4	6.7	5.1	6.9	7.9	7.4
Unit	10.2	9.8	9.8	8.7	9.8	8.1	9.7	10.6	8.5

[a]Annual indices are the predicted value from the trend analysis plus the deviation from the expected value in a year.
Large but nonsignificant changes due to small sample sizes produce exaggerated indices over the 36-year period.
[b] New England consists of CT, ME, MA, NH, RI, and VT.
[c] Ohio became a hunting state in 1995.

16

Table 3. Trends (% change[a] per year as determined by linear regression) in number of mourning doves heard along Breeding Bird Survey routes, 1966-2000.

	10 year (1991-00)				35 year (1966-00)				
	N	% Change		90% CI		N	% Change		90% CI	
EASTERN UNIT										
Hunt										
AL	87	0.1		-1.4	1.6	91	-1.1	**	-1.8	-0.4
DE/MD	72	-0.6		-2.1	0.9	81	0.6		-0.0	1.2
FL	84	-0.4		-1.7	1.0	97	2.6	***	1.7	3.5
GA	62	-2.8	***	-4.3	-1.4	68	-1.2	**	-2.1	-0.3
IL	82	0.9		-0.3	2.2	82	0.5		-0.4	1.3
IN	52	-1.2		-2.6	0.2	53	-0.2		-0.8	0.4
KY	38	0.2		-1.3	1.8	50	0.4		-0.3	1.0
LA	54	3.5	**	1.0	6.1	69	1.8	**	0.5	3.1
MS	30	-3.7	*	-6.8	-0.6	40	-1.4	**	-2.3	-0.5
NC	67	-0.4		-1.5	0.7	77	-0.4		-1.1	0.4
OH[c]	74	0.5		-0.7	1.7	83	0.7	*	0.0	1.3
PA	104	2.0	**	0.6	3.4	124	2.4	***	1.7	3.1
SC	29	3.7	**	1.3	6.1	35	-0.2		-1.1	0.7
TN	44	-0.7		-2.8	1.3	48	-0.8		-1.8	0.3
VA	71	-0.1		-1.8	1.6	77	-0.5		-1.1	0.1
WV	53	3.0		-0.3	6.4	58	5.9	***	4.9	6.8
Subunit	1003	-0.1		-0.6	0.4	1133	0.1		-0.2	0.4
Nonhunt										
MI	74	1.3	**	0.3	2.3	84	0.4		-0.2	1.0
N.England[d]	142	1.1		-0.1	2.4	154	3.8	***	2.8	4.7
NJ	29	0.6		-1.9	3.1	36	0.7		-0.6	2.0
NY	106	2.4	***	1.1	3.8	115	3.1	***	2.6	3.6
WI	87	0.8		-0.4	2.0	89	1.1	*	0.0	2.1
Subunit	438	1.3	***	0.7	1.9	478	1.8	***	1.4	2.3
Unit	1441	0.2		-0.3	0.6	1611	0.5	***	0.2	0.7
CENTRAL UNIT										
AR	34	3.4	***	1.9	4.9	37	0.1		-1.1	1.2
CO	117	3.3	***	1.8	4.9	122	1.1	*	0.0	2.2
IA	36	0.8		-1.0	2.7	37	-0.9	*	-1.8	-0.0
KS	38	-1.7		-3.8	0.4	39	-0.1		-0.9	0.7
MN	64	-0.2		-2.6	2.2	71	-1.1		-2.3	0.0
MO	52	-1.4	**	-2.4	-0.3	61	-2.5	***	-3.1	-1.8
MT	51	-2.2		-4.8	0.4	58	-0.8	*	-1.4	-0.1
NE	41	-1.1		-3.0	0.7	45	-0.8	**	-1.5	-0.2
NM	63	0.3		-2.3	2.8	70	-0.8		-2.6	1.0
ND	44	-3.2	***	-4.7	-1.6	46	1.5	***	0.9	2.0
OK	58	-0.5		-2.3	1.2	63	-1.7	***	-2.4	-1.0
SD	44	-2.0		-4.3	0.4	54	0.6		-0.2	1.4
TX	169	-0.5		-1.9	0.8	188	-1.6	***	-2.2	-1.0
WY	77	-1.7		-4.4	1.0	98	-0.4		-1.6	0.8
Unit	888	-0.5		-1.1	0.1	989	-0.7	***	-0.9	-0.4
WESTERN UNIT										
AZ	61	-0.3		-2.8	2.1	74	-1.2		-3.2	0.8
CA	170	0.6		-1.0	2.2	214	-1.1	***	-1.8	-0.4
ID	45	-0.7		-3.6	2.2	48	-1.7	***	-2.6	-0.8
NV	27	7.1	***	3.6	10.7	35	4.4	**	1.3	7.4
OR	83	4.9	**	1.4	8.4	98	-2.2	**	-3.8	-0.7
UT	87	1.0		-1.4	3.4	89	-2.3	**	-3.7	-0.8
WA	60	0.3		-2.4	3.1	68	0.1		-1.8	2.0
Unit	533	1.0		0.0	2.0	626	-1.3	***	-1.8	-0.7

[a] Mean of route trends weighted by land area and population density. The estimated count in the next year is (%/100+1) times the count in the current year where % is the annual change. Note: Extrapolating the estimated trend statistic (% change per year) over time (e.g., 35 years) may exaggerate the total change over the period.
[b] $*P<0.1$; $**P<0.05$; $***P<0.01$.
[c] Ohio became a hunting state in 1995.
[d] New England consists of CT, ME, MA, NH, RI, and VT.

17

Table 4. The number of days afield, birds bagged, active hunters, the bag per active hunter and percent confidence intervals for each from the 1999-00 Harvest Information Program harvest surveys.

State	Days afield	95%CI	Birds bagged	95%CI	Active hunters	95%CI	Bag/Active hunter	95%CI
Alabama	181,000	12%	1,320,600	16%	57,300	8%	23	18%
Arkansas	130,100	17%	950,900	18%	35,600	11%	27	21%
Arizona	97,800	11%	633,600	14%	30,500	7%	21	15%
California	168,700	12%	800,700	12%	56,400	10%	14	15%
Colorado	42,600	19%	221,400	20%	14,200	15%	16	26%
Delaware	13,300	32%	88000	32%	3,700	32%	24	45%
Florida	76,000	28%	515,600	33%	18,100	21%	28	40%
Georgia	141,500	14%	972,700	17%	46,900	10%	21	20%
Idaho	24,600	21%	87,000	20%	7,300	17%	12	26%
Illinois	106,800	13%	538,100	15%	31,200	10%	17	19%
Indiana	53,800	31%	279,200	27%	14,000	19%	20	34%
Kansas	151,600	12%	757,100	13%	36,300	8%	21	15%
Kentucky	110,000	34%	911,600	47%	33,500	16%	27	50%
Louisiana	119,500	21%	845,900	25%	40,100	18%	21	31%
Maryland	19,900	30%	106,200	28%	5,400	28%	20	40%
Mississippi	75,300	14%	607,000	18%	27,700	12%	22	22%
Missouri	108,800	14%	598,900	18%	35,500	11%	17	21%
Montana	3,800	74%	18,700	77%	1,200	72%	15	105%
North Carolina	177,800	23%	1,112,000	22%	64,900	17%	17	28%
North Dakota	22,300	23%	111,300	25%	6,200	25%	18	35%
Nebraska	75,400	13%	308,200	14%	19,200	10%	16	17%
New Mexico	34,500	43%	157,000	56%	7,400	36%	21	66%
Nevada	13,800	50%	64,400	67%	4,100	26%	16	71%
Ohio	89,700	18%	295,700	20%	20,300	16%	15	26%
Oklahoma	133,800	12%	713,900	11%	37,200	8%	19	13%
Oregon	21,400	31%	75,100	34%	5,900	27%	13	44%
Pennsylvania	176,000	13%	601,500	17%	39,900	10%	15	20%
Rhode Island	1,100	79%	6,000	102%	300	65%	20	121%
South Carolina	132,100	14%	868,800	16%	37,000	10%	23	19%
South Dakota	40,600	22%	185,900	22%	10,900	21%	17	30%
Tennessee	95,600	42%	420,300	26%	31,700	23%	13	35%
Texas	1,301,900	7%	7,416,400	7%	297,500	5%	25	9%
Utah	23,700	15%	73,600	15%	8,800	16%	8	22%
Virginia	65,700	16%	338,800	16%	23,400	11%	14	19%
Washington	28,100	29%	96,300	28%	11,000	23%	9	37%
West Virginia	10,500	138%	13,200	71%	2,200	69%	6	98%
Wyoming	6,100	27%	23,600	25%	2,900	47%	8	53%

18

Table 5. The number of days afield, birds bagged, active hunters, the bag per active hunter and percent confidence intervals for each from the 2000-01 Harvest Information Program harvest surveys.

State	Days afield	95%CI	Birds bagged	95%CI	Active hunters	95%CI	Bag/Active hunter	95%CI
Alabama	161,200	17%	1,132,700	18%	57,200	11%	20	21%
Arkansas	128,600	16%	944,700	17%	38,600	12%	25	21%
Arizona	96,100	11%	602,000	15%	30,800	9%	20	17%
California	187,500	16%	995,100	16%	56,100	11%	18	19%
Colorado	45,500	20%	242,600	21%	16,300	17%	15	27%
Delaware	8,300	31%	64500	42%	2,500	29%	26	51%
Florida	96,000	88%	577,200	88%	20,400	53%	28	103%
Georgia	143,600	11%	994,000	13%	43,800	9%	23	16%
Idaho	20,600	27%	78,400	23%	6,000	18%	13	30%
Illinois	136,900	17%	764,800	14%	35,000	11%	22	18%
Indiana	52,200	26%	278,800	25%	14,300	19%	20	32%
Kansas	148,200	12%	831,700	14%	35,800	9%	23	17%
Kentucky	107,800	28%	740,500	33%	32,900	23%	23	40%
Louisiana	104,600	27%	740,700	34%	30,100	17%	25	38%
Maryland	42,200	40%	190,700	27%	13,900	30%	14	41%
Mississippi	74,100	15%	630,600	18%	25,600	13%	25	22%
Missouri	111,400	19%	570,000	23%	30,100	13%	19	27%
Montana	2,300	66%	9,300	93%	1,100	82%	9	124%
North Carolina	190,600	20%	1,072,700	20%	64,900	15%	17	25%
North Dakota	16,700	26%	65,200	31%	4,800	32%	14	44%
Nebraska	68,700	12%	325,900	11%	19,200	10%	17	15%
New Mexico	43,000	25%	263,100	32%	9,600	18%	27	37%
Nevada	12,600	33%	75,300	45%	4,200	29%	18	53%
Ohio	130,800	22%	476,400	29%	32,500	18%	15	34%
Oklahoma	78,800	33%	631,600	47%	18,200	32%	35	57%
Oregon	20,900	40%	69,200	36%	6,800	29%	10	46%
Pennsylvania	147,300	17%	453,500	17%	34,500	11%	13	20%
Rhode Island	500	71%	1,500	92%	100	61%	11	110%
South Carolina	129,600	16%	812,500	18%	34,300	13%	24	22%
South Dakota	27,100	24%	156,100	34%	8,100	25%	19	42%
Tennessee	109,300	33%	903,500	47%	43,600	30%	21	56%
Texas	1,390,000	7%	9,018,600	8%	343,900	5%	26	9%
Utah	29,500	18%	119,600	19%	10,900	16%	11	25%
Virginia	89,400	17%	423,100	20%	27,400	12%	15	23%
Washington	21,400	30%	84,900	25%	8,500	30%	10	39%
West Virginia	7,200	68%	34,600	101%	1,300	38%	26	108%
Wyoming	8,000	37%	44,000	41%	4,100	40%	11	57%

Harvest Dynamics of Mourning Doves in South Carolina

JAMES B. BERDEEN, Department of Aquaculture, Fisheries, and Wildlife, Lehotsky Hall, Clemson University, Clemson, SC 29634

DAVID L. OTIS, U.S. Geological Survey, Biological Resources Division, South Carolina Cooperative Fish and Wildlife Research Unit, Lehotsky Hall, Clemson University, Clemson, SC 29634

Graduate student: James B. Berdeen (Ph.D.); **Expected completion:** December 2001

Call-count surveys indicate the mourning dove (*Zenaida macroura*) population in South Carolina and the Eastern Management Unit (EMU) declined from 1991-2000 (Smith and Dolton 2000). Although reasons for this negative trend are not known, annual survival, particularly of juveniles, appears to have decreased in South Carolina between the 1970's and 1990's (Haas 1978, McGowan and Otis 1998). Thus, there is a need for investigations into the patterns of mortality rates at times during the annual cycle when mortality is thought to be particularly high.

The role that various sources of direct mortality and their interactions have played in the population dynamics of mourning doves is sometimes unclear (Braun et al. 1993). Because South Carolina is thought to have had a high harvest rate historically (Shipes et al. 1983) and the role of hunting in this population decline is unknown, we examined population parameters on 3 sites with different levels of hunting pressure in the Coastal Plain of South Carolina to address hypotheses of compensatory mortality.

The objectives of this study are to: (1) estimate cause-specific mortality rates from July-November, (2) determine whether site-, year-, and age-specific differences in period survival rates exist, (3) compare harvest rate estimates of derived from banding and telemetry data, (4) estimate the crippling rate of doves, and (5) examine the influence of various abiotic factors on indices of annual production, (6) assess the impact of subcutaneously implanted radiotransmitters on the health and survival of doves.

We are using telemetry and banding data to estimate period and annual survival rates, respectively. Telemetry data are also being used to estimate the magnitude and timing of various sources of mortality, and to estimate crippling rates. We are collecting harvest age ratio data at organized dove hunts within 5 km of the 3 study sites. This 5 km buffer zone surrounding the core study sites defines the boundaries of each study site.

We elected to attach radiotransmitters to birds using the subcutaneous implantation method (Schulz et al. 1998) because, in general, traditional methods of radiomarking mourning doves have been unsuccessful. During Fall 1997, we began meeting with Clemson University (CU) veterinarians to acquire their assistance in the surgical implantation of transmitters during the 1998 field season. Because the veterinarians were unfamiliar with this marking technique and unsure of the health effects on the birds, the University Animal Research Committee (ARC) required us to conduct a pilot study to determine whether the radiomarked birds developed any negative health effects. The ARC permitted us to initiate field research upon the successful completion of the pilot study.

We captured doves in Kniffin traps baited with corn, wheat, sorghum, browntop millet, and/or proso millet. We classified the age and gender of captured doves (Table 1), and held birds in outdoor cages for up to 4 days before they were transported to a veterinary facility to be implanted with a transmitter. Implantationsurgeries were performed at Clemson University in 1998, and at a veterinary clinic near our study area in 1999 and 2000. Birds were held in captivity $\geq$36 hours, then released. In 1998, we released radiomarked birds at the exact points of capture throughout the diurnal period. Unfortunately, 6 birds were predated within 2 days of release. Suspected predators were hawks, owls, and red foxes.

Although we considered the subcutaneous implantation of transmitters to have been successful, we modified our methods of releasing radiomarked birds back into the wild in 1999 and 2000. We released radiomarked birds in microhabitats near the point of capture in which predators would have more difficulty foraging, provided concentrations of preferred foods at the capture site, and released birds in the early morning before buteo hawks could hunt on thermal air currents and when owls were not active. The number of radiotagged birds predated within 7 days of release was reduced to 2 and 5 in 1999 and 2000, respectively.

In 1998, 8 birds (4 juveniles, 3 adult males, and 1 individual of unknown age and gender) were harvested by hunters on the heavily hunted site. On the lightly hunted site, 1 juvenile was taken by a raptor and 5 birds (2 juveniles, 1 adult male, 1 adult female, and 1 adult of unknown gender) were taken by hunters. On the non-hunted site, 1 juvenile was predated by a raptor, 1 bird of unknown age or gender was predated by a mammal, 2 birds (1 juvenile and 1 bird of unknown age and gender) were harvested by hunters, and 1 adult male was thought to be scavenged by a mammal after being shot but not retrieved. In 1999, 1 juvenile was predated by a raptor and 10 birds (4 juveniles, 3 adult males, and 3 birds of unknown age and gender) were harvested by hunters on the heavily hunted site. One adult male was predated by a raptor on the lightly hunted site. One adult male was predated by a raptor and another adult male was shot but not retrieved near the non-hunted site. As of mid-November 2000, 4 birds (3 juveniles and 1 adult of unidentified gender) had been harvested by hunters on the heavily hunted site. Six birds (3 adult males, 1 adult of unidentified gender, and 2 juveniles) were taken by hunters on the lightly hunted site. Near the nonhunted site, 1 juvenile was harvested by a hunter, 1 juvenile was predated by a raptor, and 2 birds were predated by unidentified predators.

Preliminary analyses indicate that the July - November period survival rates of adults were 0.71 (0.530 - 0.895, 95% CI), 0.73 (0.530- 0.916), and 0.75 (0.569-0.927) in 1998, 1999, and 2000, respectively. Juveniles had period survival rates of 0.43 (0.172-0.691), 0.54 (0.235-0.837), and 0.54 (0.319-0.763) in 1998, 1999, and 2000, respectively. We did not know the fate of 36 and 61% of the doves in the 1998 and 1999 field seasons, respectively, and expect to right-censor a similar proportion of our radiomarked population at the end of the 2000 field season. Possible explanations for the loss of these birds include migration from the study area, transmitter failure, and hunters not reporting harvested birds with transmitters.

We attended dove hunts that occurred within 5 km of the boundaries of each core study site to search for radiomarked doves that were harvested and to ascertain the age ratio of harvested birds. This ratio serves as an index of annual production. The uncorrected age ratios (juveniles:adult) of harvested birds were 2.34:1, 1.88:1, and 2.46:1 in 1998, 1999, and 2000, respectively. These production indices are well below those previously documented in the Carolinas (Haas 1978, McGowan and Otis 1998). Because the factors responsible for annual variation in this ratio are unknown, we will explore the relationship between weather patterns and the corrected age ratios of harvested doves from 4 studies (Hayne 1975, Haas 1978, McGowan and Otis 1998, this study) conducted in the Carolinas.

Funding for this study was provided by the 1996 and 2000 Webless Migratory Game Bird Research Program (U.S. Fish and Wildlife Service and U.S. Geological Survey - Biological Resources Division) South Carolina Department of Natural Resources, South Carolina Public Service Authority (Santee-Cooper), Clemson University, Safari Club International, and the South Carolina Cooperative Fish and Wildlife Research Unit.

Table 1. Sample sizes of site-, year-, and age-sex classes of radiomarked mourning doves, Coastal Plain of South Carolina, 1998-2000.

Site	Year	AHY-M	AHY-F	AHY-U	HY-U	U-U
Heavily-hunted	1998	11	1	0	15	4
	1999	15	2	0	14	5
	2000	7	0	3	13	4
Lightly-hunted	1998	7	6	2	5	2
	1999	12	2	1	10	2
	2000	10	3	1	11	2
Nonhunted	1998	9	4	0	12	5
	1999	8	2	2	11	3
	2000	5	9	1	11	4

Monitoring the Presence and Annual Variation of *Trichomonas gallinae* in Mourning Dove Populations

JOHN H. SCHULZ, Missouri Department of Conservation, Fish and Wildlife Research Center, 1110 S. College Ave, Columbia, MO 65201

ALEX J. BERMUDEZ, University of Missouri, Veterinary Medicine Diagnostic Laboratory, Columbia, MO 65211

JOHN FISCHER, University of Georgia, Southeastern Cooperative Wildlife Disease Study, Athens, GA 30602

Expected completion date: June 2002

Trichomonas gallinae is a pear-shaped flagellated protozoan which sometimes causes a fatal disease called trichomoniasis in mourning doves and other columbids. The disease is thought to be transmitted when infected adults feed nestlings, and/or contaminate drinking water and food sources (i.e., bird feeders or baths). Weather conditions may contribute to disease transmission; e.g., extended hot dry weather may force birds to use limited but contaminated food and water supplies. Trichomonads are usually found in the oral-nasal cavity, or anterior end of the digestive and respiratory tracts of infected birds. Symptoms include difficulty flying, listlessness, swollen necks, and cheesy yellowish lesions in the oral cavity. Death occurs when the lesions block the trachea and oral cavity making eating and respiration impossible. Our objectives are to determine the presence of *Trichomonas gallinae* in a local mourning dove population using hunter killed birds on the James A. Reed Memorial Wildlife Area (JARMWA), Missouri, 1998-2002, and to evaluate the practicality of a large scale *Trichomonas gallinae* monitoring program to monitor trends in the disease's presence through time. Our goal is to attempt to sample 1,000 hunter killed birds annually using the InPouch® TF (BioMed Diagnostics, San Jose, CA, USA) culture system for detecting trichomonads. Using 3 captive mourning doves from another study, which died from trichomoniasis, we tested how long trichomonads lived in the dead birds. Viable trichomonads were found >36 hrs after the birds died and were left at ambient temperature showing that hunter killed birds would prove useful in detecting the presence of the parasite.

During 1 September 1998, we tested 687 hunter killed doves from JARMWA; an additional 29 doves were sampled from Eagle Bluff Conservation Area during the first and third days of the hunting season to increase our sample size. Of the 716 birds sampled, none showed visible lesions but 39 (5.4%) tested positive for carrying the parasite. During 1 September 1999, we tested 541 hunter killed birds from JARMWA. Of the 541 birds sampled, no birds showed visible lesions but 30 (5.5%) tested positive for carrying the parasite. During 1 September 2000, we tested only 415; we sampled fewer birds because of extremely hot weather on opening day of the dove season and corresponding low hunter participation. None of the 415 birds showed visible lesions; however, 10.6% of the birds tested positive for carrying the parasite. Given the relatively low cost of this study, we are considering continuing this project beyond 2002. A longer term monitoring program would provide more insights into annual variation in the presence of the disease, and more certainty concerning factors that relate to causes of the annual variation.

These preliminary results represent the third year of a 4-year study. The final report for the first 4 years study will be available by June 2002. Funding for this study was provided by 1998 Webless Migratory Game Bird Research Program (U.S. Fish and Wildlife Service and the U.S. Geological Survey-Biological Resources Division), and the Missouri Department of Conservation-Conservation Research Center (Federal Aid in Wildlife Restoration Project W-13-R-52).

Lead Exposure in Mourning Doves

J. CHRISTIAN FRANSON, U.S. Geological Survey, Biological Resources Division, National Wildlife Health Center, 6006 Schroeder Rd, Madison, WI 53711

Expected Completion: December 2000

Regulations restricting the use of lead shot have been enacted in North America and Europe, primarily because of waterfowl mortality due to lead shot ingestion. In the United States, lead shot was banned for use in waterfowl hunting in 1991, but there has been concern about the extent to which upland birds are being exposed to lead shot. Lead exposure from the ingestion of spent lead shot has been documented in several species of North American upland game birds, including the mourning dove (*Zenaida macroura*). Mourning doves are frequently harvested in selectively managed fields, where up to five to eight shotshells are expended per bird taken, resulting in lead shot densities of greater than 860,000 pellets per hectare being reported from heavily hunted dove fields. Ingestion of lead shot by mourning doves may lead to lead poisoning and death, and lead exposure may cause sublethal physiological or behavioral effects that could result in starvation, the inability to escape from predators, or perhaps an increased susceptibility to disease. Although the mourning dove is a species of special concern regarding lead exposure and information on lead poisoning has been identified as a research need for proper dove population management, data on lead shot ingestion and lead concentrations in tissues of mourning doves are limited. Studies have been conducted in several states, but sample sizes varied widely and study designs have differed. The objective of this study is to evaluate the prevalence of lead exposure in mourning doves, based on ingested lead shot and lead concentrations in liver and bone, in a sample of hunter-killed birds from the three primary management units. The prevalence of ingested lead shot in gizzards will provide an index to the frequency with which mourning doves are picking up lead shot, and lead residues in liver and bone will reflect recent and chronic lead exposure, respectively.

During September 1998 and 1999, a total of 4,415 hunter-killed doves was collected in seven states: Arizona, Missouri, Pennsylvania, South Carolina, Tennessee, Georgia, and Oklahoma. All carcasses were aged and sexed, and gizzards, livers, and wing bones were removed. The gizzards were radiographed and examined visually for the presence of shot. Shot-in and ingested shot were differentiated by the presence or absence of entry wounds in the gizzard and physical characteristics of the shot. Of the 4,415 doves collected in 1998 and 1999, we found ingested shot in 1.8% of the gizzards, while 2.2% of the gizzards contained shot-in shot. As of November 2000, livers from 1,975 doves have been analyzed for lead. Our results indicate that 6.5% of these doves had been exposed to lead, using the commonly accepted criterion of • 6.0 parts per million (dry weight) of lead in the liver as an indicator of exposure. During September 2000, 170 additional carcasses were collected in Arizona. These carcasses will be processed as described above, resulting in a total sample size of nearly 4,600 doves over the three field seasons covered by the study. Final results will include the frequency of lead shot ingestion in the mourning doves collected during the study and data summarizing lead residues in liver and bone from a sub-sample of carcasses.

These results are from the third year of a 4-year study funded by the 1998 Webless Migratory Game Bird Research Program (U.S. Fish and Wildlife Service), Arizona Game and Fish Department, Georgia Department of Natural Resources, Oklahoma Department of Wildlife Conservation, Missouri Department of Conservation, Pennsylvania Game Commission, South Carolina Department of Natural Resources, and the Tennessee Wildlife Resources Agency. Additional cooperators include the South Carolina Cooperative Fish and Wildlife Research Unit. During the year 2001, we will finish the laboratory work and prepare the final report, which we expect to be completed by December, 2001.

Development and Evaluation of Mourning Dove Population Models for Optimizing Harvest Management Strategies in the Eastern Management Unit, Central Management Unit, and Western Management Unit

DAVID L. OTIS, U.S. Geological Survey, Biological Resources Division, South Carolina Cooperative Fish and Wildlife Research Unit, Lehotsky Hall, Clemson University, Clemson, SC 29634

Expected completion: June 2004

Despite the fact that mourning doves are among the ten most ubiquitous and numerous bird species in the continental U.S. (Robbins et. al 1986), indices of population density have been declining during the past 30 years. The Call Count Survey (CCS) reveals significant declines in all management units during the periods 1966-2000 and 1991-2000 (Dolton and Smith 2000). The Breeding Bird Survey (BBS) indicates similarly significant declines in the Central Management Unit (CMU) and the Western Management Unit (WMU), but not in the Eastern Management Unit (EMU), during approximately the same time periods (Sauer et al. 1997). The BBS also shows significant declines in the continental U.S. (Sauer et al. 1997).

The breeding ecology of mourning doves has been well studied, and many local and relatively short term studies have produced estimates of various measures of productivity (Sayre and Silvy 1993). However, in contrast to the situation for such species as woodcock and waterfowl, for which annual age ratio data are collected in wing surveys of hunters on a continental

scale, no annual program for producing indices of breeding success or productivity is conducted in the U.S. for doves. A few studies have included collection of harvest age ratio data (Hayne 1975; Haas 1978; McGowan and Otis 1998), but these have been relatively short term (5-6 years) and small scale efforts. Moreover, no accepted models have been developed that relate such factors as weather or land use conditions to annual productivity. Thus, current indices of reproduction are not available from any source on a management unit scale.

Banding studies dating back to the 1950's have been used to generate annual mortality estimates (Newsom et al. 1957, Tomlinson et al. 1960). The most recent estimates of mortality on a management unit scale were derived from the intensive banding studies carried out in each management unit in the 1960's and 1970's (Dunks et al. 1982, Tomlinson et al. 1988, Martin and Sauer 1993). Aside from a few small scale banding studies in South Carolina (McGowan and Otis 1998), California (M. R. Miller pers. comm.), Ohio (D. Scott pers. comm.) and a proposed project in Missouri

(J. H. Schulz pers. comm.), no new annual mortality estimates have been generated for dove populations during the past 2 decades. Fewer than 1000 doves are banded each year in the entire U.S., and recovery rates are negligible (K. A. Wilkins, USFWS, pers. comm.). Thus, generation of contemporary annual mortality rates based on band recovery data is not feasible.

Prior to implementation of the U.S. Fish and Wildlife Service Harvest Information Program (HIP) in 1992, there was no coordinated national survey for collecting dove harvest statistics. Harvest information was collected in some individual states using mail or telephone surveys of hunting license holders, but each survey was designed independently depending on circumstances and objectives in each state. With the complete implementation of HIP in 1998, annual estimates of harvest and effort will be available for all states.

Annual mortality estimates of adult and juvenile age classes can be used to calculate an estimate of annual productivity required to maintain a stable population . These estimates can in turn be compared to available estimates of productivity to gain a sense of whether the annual cycle of mortality and natality are in balance. This procedure, followed by Dunks et al. (1982) and Tomlinson et al. (1988) on the data generated from the 1960's and 1970's banding studies in the CMU and WMU, led to the conclusion that the relation between productivity and mortality was consistent with the hypothesis of stable population levels. In addition, Hayne (1975) found no negative effects of increased bag limits on EMU populations. In the 1980's, a concern about effects of early September hunting on dove reproduction led to a study that subsequently concluded that effects were negligible (Geissler et al. 1987).

The collective result of previous studies have arguably been responsible for the lack of active dove harvest management during the past 25 years, and the lack of support for development and implementation of a more rigorous and coordinated monitoring program. A notable exception has occurred relatively recently in the WMU, where harvest restrictions were imposed in 1987 due to a concern about the steady, long term decline in the WMU CCS index. Mourning dove hunting regulation frameworks have been stable in the short term (5-10 years), but gradually liberalized in the

long term (20-30 years; Tomlinson et al. 1994, Reeves 1993) concurrent with nationwide human population growth and changes in land use and habitat fragmentation at the landscape scale.

In the past few years, several groups have begun calling for development of a more active and rigorous harvest management strategy for doves (e.g., CMU Mourning Dove Management Guidelines, CMU Mourning Dove Workshop Proposal, USFWS Migratory Bird Management Office). These documents all describe the need to develop one or more population models to predict effects of different harvest prescriptions on long term population and harvest levels, and ultimately define decision criteria for implementing these alternative harvest strategies. Such a modeling effort would represent an initial step in a process to an improved decision making process for mourning doves, and would begin to place mourning dove harvest management in an objective and quantitative framework.

Expected Benefits

Understanding the effects of harvest on mourning dove populations is a multi-faceted challenge, and this effort is only one of many steps in increasing our knowledge. Upon completion of the project, we expect to have advanced the process of developing an improved system of dove harvest management by 1) improving our understanding of dove population dynamics, 2) prioritizing population monitoring data needs within the context of a long term harvest management system, and 3) recommending surveys and studies to fill information gaps that constrain development of more useful and realistic population models.

Methods

Contemporary information about dove population demographics and the relationship of mortality and reproductive rates to extrinsic and intrinsic factors is clearly inadequate to support sophisticated modeling fitting or adaptive modeling efforts at this point in time. However, it is necessary to begin development and evaluation of rudimentary models that represent a first step toward a long term objective of improved dove harvest management strategies that are grounded in credible population models and that guide improved population monitoring programs that will be necessary to support management efforts.

The proposed elements of the study are as follows:

1) Use historical band recovery data, harvest age ratio data, and auxiliary information as appropriate to develop simple structural models of annual survival and reproduction. Specifically, the relationship between survival and harvest rate will be explored using, for example, ultrastructure models (Burnham et al. 1984) and band recovery data from large scale banding studies conducted in the 1960's and 1970's. Estimated preseason age ratios will be modeled as functions of environmental variables which will vary with geographical region.

2) Structural equations developed in #1) will be used as the basis for development of a small set of population life cycle models for each of the 3 management units, and possibly subunits demonstrating significant CCS trend declines.

3) A range of plausible parameters values, based on historical literature, will be used to investigate the sensitivity of predicted population trajectories to change in individual parameters, including harvest rates.

4) On a regional or management unit scale, predicted population trajectories from different models will be compared to CCS trends, as a coarse check on model validity.

5) Based on sensitivity modeling results, recommendations will be made regarding the need for contemporary estimates of population parameters, and associated sample sizes necessary to achieve desired precision.

Progress to Date

Re-analysis of the 1965 -1975 banding experiment on increased bag limits in the EMU has been completed and a manuscript submitted for publication. The analysis revealed that the increase in bag limits during experimental years did not result in increased harvest rates, and thus the study could not provide any rigorous insight into the relationship between harvest and annual survival. There was a high degree of association between annual survival rates from banding data and harvest rate estimates derived from mail survey data collected during the study. Dove populations from groups of non-hunting states in the Northeast and Upper Mideast had much higher annual survival rates. However, this phenomenon can also be at least partially explained by a hypothesis of an intrinsic latitudinal gradient in annual survival of mourning doves.

Re-analysis of the 1965-1975 banding studies in the CMU and WMU is nearly complete. Historical harvest age ratio data and estimates of reproduction from the literature are being compiled as a first step in development of reproductive sub-models.

This study is being funded by the Webless Migratory Game Bird Research Program, a consortium of state wildlife agencies, and the U.S. Fish and Wildlife Service (Division of Migratory Bird Management).

Mourning Dove Hunting in Alabama: Motivations, Satisfactions, and Sociocultural Influences

STEVEN E. HAYSLETTE, School of Forestry and Wildlife Sciences, 108 M. White Smith Hall, Auburn University, AL 36849-5418
JAMES B. ARMSTRONG, School of Forestry and Wildlife Sciences, 108 M. White Smith Hall, Auburn University, AL 36849-5418
RALPH E. MIRARCHI, Center for Forest Sustainability, School of Forestry and Wildlife Sciences, 108 M. White Smith Hall, Auburn University, AL 36849-5418

Graduate student: Steven E. Hayslette (Ph.D.); **Final report**

Knowledge of factors affecting participation in, and satisfactions gained from, hunting is important yet unstudied among mourning dove hunters. We tested the multiple-satisfactions model of hunting and investigated effects of motivational factors and sociocultural characteristics on development and maintenance of dove hunting behavior using a mail survey of hunters in Alabama.

Most Alabama hunters appeared motivated by multiple, primarily non-success-based, satisfactions. Dove hunters were more strongly motivated by non-success-based satisfactions and less by obtaining a bag limit than were other types of hunters. Childhood socialization was important in developing hunting behavior among both dove and non-dove hunters. Early initiation into hunting and family tradition and mentoring were particularly important in developing dove hunting behavior. Attrition from dove hunting was low (<20%), and was positively associated with currently living in an urban area, but was unrelated to other sociocultural variables or to motivational factors. Management for multiple hunting satisfactions seems appropriate, given the importance of non-success-based motivations and satisfactions. Lack of family tradition and mentoring may limit success of youth programs encouraging hunting.

These are final results from this study; a manuscript has been prepared and submitted for publication. Funding was provided by the Alabama Department of Conservation and Natural Resources (Division of Wildlife and Freshwater Fisheries) and Auburn University.

Hunter Opinions Regarding Mourning Dove Management on Alabama Public Lands

STEVEN E. HAYSLETTE, School of Forestry and Wildlife Sciences, 108 M. White Smith Hall, Auburn University, AL 36849-5418
JAMES B. ARMSTRONG, School of Forestry and Wildlife Sciences, 108 M. White Smith Hall, Auburn University, AL 36849-5418
RALPH E. MIRARCHI, Center for Forest Sustainability, School of Forestry and Wildlife Sciences, 108 M. White Smith Hall, Auburn University, AL 36849-5418

Graduate student: Steven E. Hayslette (Ph.D.); **Final report**

The importance of public lands for mourning dove (*Zenaida macroura*) hunting in the Southeast may increase as other dove hunting opportunities decrease, and maximizing satisfaction of dove hunters on these lands requires knowledge concerning hunter opinions and preferences. We documented dove hunter satisfaction on state Wildlife Management Areas (WMAs) in Alabama with respect to habitat and hunter management.

Crops planted were the primary management concern; hunters preferred corn and browntop millet for dove hunting. Most dove hunters encountered unsafe conditions primarily blamed on crowding, but safety problems detracted little from overall hunting satisfaction. Hunters generally were satisfied with regulation enforcement and season starting date. Low success or perceived likelihood of success did not appear responsible for a low percentage of dove hunters using WMAs, and these factors seemed unimportant to overall satisfaction. Hunter density on dove fields should be limited to assure safety, and hunter education should emphasize safety issues associated with dove hunting. Planting browntop millet and corn in dove fields may increase hunter satisfaction on WMAs, but we recommend improved public relation programs that educate hunters regarding dove hunting safety, dove food preferences, and dove nutritional needs.

These are final results from this study; a manuscript has been prepared and submitted for publication. Funding was provided by the Alabama Department of Conservation and Natural Resources (Division of Wildlife and Freshwater Fisheries) and Auburn University.

Mourning Doves and Salt: Is There an Attraction?

STEVEN E. HAYSLETTE, School of Forestry and Wildlife Sciences, 108 M. White Smith Hall, Auburn University, AL 36849-5418

RALPH E. MIRARCHI, Center for Forest Sustainability, School of Forestry and Wildlife Sciences, 108 M. White Smith Hall, Auburn University, AL 36849-5418

Graduate student: Steven E. Hayslette (Ph.D.); **Final report**

Baiting with sodium salt to attract mourning doves (*Zenaida macroura*) for hunting has been illegal since 1931, yet no comprehensive study of the relationship between mourning doves and salt in the environment has been conducted. We measured consumption of freely available salt by captive male and female mourning doves, and we tested effects of season, grit availability, and reproductive status on salt consumption. Additionally, we evaluated the attraction of wild mourning doves to salt by comparing dove use among resource patches containing food and salt baits, salt bait, food bait, and no bait at 2 sites in east-central Alabama.

Captive doves consumed 20 ± 3 (• ± SE) mg salt/day. Salt consumption did not vary between genders, among seasons, or with availability of another grit source. Grit consumption by females during April-May was greater than during other periods, and greater than males during any period. Pairs of doves successfully hatching young consumed more salt/dove/day than did unsuccessful pairs or unpaired doves. Among successful nesters, mean salt consumption was highest during the week following hatching. Wild mourning dove use was similar between patches containing both food and salt and those containing food, and between patches containing salt and unbaited patches. Results confirm that mourning doves will consume salt in their environment, particularly during nesting, apparently in response to physiological demand for sodium. However, salt did not appear to attract wild mourning doves, perhaps due to physiological sodium-conserving mechanisms or the availability of natural sodium sources. Neither does salt appear to function as grit in the diet of mourning doves. Grit may be an important source of calcium for doves during reproduction. Regulations prohibiting salt baiting for dove hunting may not be necessary, although additional research should be conducted in other areas to validate our results.

These are final results from this study; a manuscript has been prepared and submitted for publication. Funding was provided by the Alabama Department of Conservation and Natural Resources (Division of Wildlife and Freshwater Fisheries), U.S. Fish and Wildlife Service, and Auburn University.

Do Mourning Doves Select Foods Based on Nutritional Content?

STEVEN E. HAYSLETTE, School of Forestry and Wildlife Sciences, 108 M. White Smith Hall, Auburn University, AL 36849-5418

RALPH E. MIRARCHI, Center for Forest Sustainability, School of Forestry and Wildlife Sciences, 108 M. White Smith Hall, Auburn University, AL 36849-5418

Graduate student: Steven E. Hayslette (Ph.D.); **Final report**

Patterns of food preference in mourning doves (*Zenaida macroura*) are not well-established, and the role of seed nutrient content in diet selection by doves is poorly understood. We documented preferences of captive and wild (free-flying) doves for foods commonly cultivated for dove habitat improvement and commonly-eaten wild foods. Additionally, we evaluated the hypothesis that food selection by doves

28

is based on nutritional content by testing predictions of changing preferences with short- and long-term (seasonal) weather changes and relationship(s) between food preferences and specific nutrients and minerals.

Captive mourning doves foraged selectively; white proso millet, dove proso millet, and browntop millet were the first, second, and third most-preferred foods, respectively. Wild doves also foraged selectively, although preferences were not as clear or strong as among captive doves. Contrary to predictions, food preferences did not vary with short-term or seasonal weather changes, and food selection was not positively related to protein, lipid, or calcium levels. Food selection was positively related to nitrogen-free extract (NFE) and negatively related to cellulose-lignin (C-L)

levels in foods, although contents of these components did not completely explain dove food selection. Seed physical characteristics, secondary compound levels, and/or metabolic efficiencies may have influenced food selection in our study. Managers should evaluate attractiveness of new foods to mourning doves based on relative NFE and C-L levels until the relationships of food attractiveness to seed physical characteristics, secondary defensive compounds, and metabolic efficiency are determined.

These are final results from this study; a manuscript has been prepared and submitted for publication. Funding was provided by the Alabama Department of Conservation and Natural Resources (Division of Wildlife and Freshwater Fisheries) and Auburn University.

Effects of Seed Weathering on Nutritional Content and Food Selection in Mourning Doves

STEVEN E. HAYSLETTE, School of Forestry and Wildlife Sciences, 108 M. White Smith Hall, Auburn University, AL 36849-5418
RALPH E. MIRARCHI, Center for Forest Sustainability, School of Forestry and Wildlife Sciences, 108 M. White Smith Hall, Auburn University, AL 36849-5418

Graduate student: Steven E. Hayslette (Ph.D.); final report; Completed: November 2000

Deterioration of seeds due to weathering may affect considerably the quantity and quality of food available for mourning doves (*Zenaida macroura*) and other granivorous wildlife through time. Deterioration rates of seeds during field weathering in terrestrial environments largely are unknown, however, and the assumed positive relationship between seed mass and nutrient losses during weathering never has been tested. Likewise, the effects of changes in seed nutrient contents during field weathering are unknown.

We documented losses of overall mass and masses of 7 nutrients in selected seeds during field weathering, and we tested the relationships between overall mass loss and loss of individual nutrients, and between overall mass loss and seed water and fiber contents. We also tested extant hypotheses regarding the roles of carbohydrate and cellulose-lignin (C-L) contents on seed selection by mourning doves by documenting

weathering-induced changes in both seed chemical content and seed selection by doves.

Most seeds lost mass during weathering; seeds of cultivated species lost mass more rapidly than those of wild species. Fat, nitrogen-free extract (NFE), protein, and hemicellulose declined in most seeds with weathering, as well. Overall mass loss in seeds was positively correlated with loss of fat, NFE, protein, ash, and water, but was not related to seed water or fiber content. Generally, mass loss appears to be a valid index of terrestrial seed deterioration. Rapid seed deterioration and/or germination may limit usefulness of cultivated species in food plantings for granivorous wildlife.

Doves selected white proso millet (*Panicum miliacium*) over all other species among fresh seeds, but selected broadleaf signalgrass (*Brachiaria platyphylla*) over all others among weathered seeds.

29

Selection among fresh seeds generally supported both hypothesized nutritional mechanisms, carbohydrate maximization and C-L minimization. Selection among weathered seeds, however, offered some support for carbohydrate maximization, but none for C-L minimization. We hypothesize that rate of energy loss, rather than energy (carbohydrate) content, determines patterns of seed selection among mourning doves. Selection for seeds losing energy most quickly may maximize long-term energy availability.

These are final results from this study; manuscripts have been prepared and submitted for publication. Funding was provided by the Alabama Department of Conservation and Natural Resources (Division of Wildlife and Freshwater Fisheries) and Auburn University.

Management of Selected Food Plantings for Mourning Doves in Alabama

STEVEN E. HAYSLETTE, School of Forestry and Wildlife Sciences, 108 M. White Smith Hall, Auburn University, AL 36849-5418

RALPH E. MIRARCHI, Center for Forest Sustainability, School of Forestry and Wildlife Sciences, 108 M. White Smith Hall, Auburn University, AL 36849-5418

Graduate student: Steven E. Hayslette (Ph.D.); Expected completion: September 2001

Changes in laws regarding acceptable planting methods in prepared mourning dove (*Zenaida macroura*) fields have created a need for improved information regarding costs and benefits of various management options. Goals of this project were to document benefits of wheat plantings for mourning doves in light of prohibition on hunting over top-sown fields, and measure and compare costs and benefits of planting strategies for highly-preferred warm-season mourning dove foods.

Field work during June-September 1998 measured and compare unshattered seed availability of experimental wheat plantings established at 3 sites in eastern Alabama during September 1997. Mean wheat seed availability in mid-June varied widely among sites. Wheat availability declined from mid-June through early August at all 3 sites, and by early August, unshattered wheat seed availability was • 0.01 g/m^2 at 2 sites. By mid-September, wheat availability at the third site had declined to <20% of that in mid-June.

Field work at these 3 sites during June-August 1998 documented and compared seed yields of experimental plantings of white proso millet, dove proso millet, browntop millet, broadleaf signalgrass (*Brachiaria platyphylla*), and yellow bristlegrass (*Setaria lutescens*). Differences in seed yield among crops varied among sites; seed yield of browntop millet was >20 times greater than yield of any other crop at 2 sites, but seed yield did not vary among crops at the third site. Yields of white proso millet and broadleaf signalgrass varied widely among sites.

Field work at the same sites during July-October 1999 tested the effects of fertilization rate on seed yield of white proso millet, dove proso millet, browntop millet, broadleaf signalgrass, yellow bristlegrass, and switchgrass (*Panicum virgatum*). We tested 4 fertilization rates, including no fertilizer; N, P, and K as recommended by soil test; twice recommended N, with P and K as recommended; and three times recommended N, with P and K as recommended. Surprisingly, seed yield did not vary among fertilization rate for any crop. Seed yield of browntop millet was >4 times greater than yield of any other species at 2 sites, and greater than that of all other species except broadleaf signalgrass at the third site. Yield of broadleaf signalgrass was greater than yield of yellow bristlegrass, white proso millet, dove proso millet, or switchgrass at 2 of the 3 sites.

Additional field work at 2 sites during July-October 1999 tested the effects of row spacing and planting rate on seed yield of white proso millet, dove proso millet, and browntop millet. We tested 3 row spacings (18, 36, and 72 cm) and 4 planting rates (5.6, 11.2, 16.8, and 22.5 kg/ha). Seed yield was greater at 36 cm row spacing than at 72 cm spacing, and was greater at planting rates of 16.8 and 22.5 kg/ha than at 5.6 kg/ha at 1 site, but seed yield did not vary among row spacings or planting rates at the second site. Seed yield of browntop millet was >4 times greater than yield of white or dove proso millets at both sites.

Results indicate that browntop millet is by far the best choice for planting in warm-season dove fields, if maximizing seed production on these fields is the desired management goal. Broadleaf signalgrass may be a cost-efficient alternative to cultivated crops for dove field plantings, if annual regeneration of signalgrass following initial establishment eliminates the need to plant each year. Results also suggest that wheat plantings provide most benefits to mourning doves early in the breeding season, and that few benefits from wheat remain by late summer. If prohibition on hunting over top-sown fields continues, wheat may be of limited use in attracting mourning doves for hunting in Alabama.

Data collection and compilation for this project is now complete, and remaining data analysis currently is underway. The final report for this project will be completed by September 2001. Funding is being provided by the Alabama Department of Conservation and Natural Resources (Division of Wildlife and Freshwater Fisheries) and Auburn University.

Nutrient Reserve Dynamics of Breeding Mourning Doves

JANICE P. HAMMER, School of Forestry and Wildlife Sciences, 108 M. White Smith Hall, Auburn University, AL 36849-5418

RALPH E. MIRARCHI, School of Forestry and Wildlife Sciences, 108 M. White Smith Hall, Auburn University, AL 36849-5418

GARY R. HEPP, School of Forestry and Wildlife Sciences, 108 M. White Smith Hall, Auburn University, AL 36849-5418

Graduate student: Janice P. Hammer (M.S.); **Final report**

Mourning Doves (*Zenaida macroura*) form strong monogamous pair bonds and produce multiple broods throughout the breeding season that typically lasts from late February to early September in Alabama. While breeding, Mourning Doves also undergo primary wing molt and begin body molt. Because body composition of Mourning Doves during the breeding season is poorly known, we determined if changes occurred in Mourning Dove body composition relative to crop gland activity phase, breeding period, and molt. We collected five adult females and five adult males per crop activity phase (active, developing/regressing, and inactive) during the breeding (early, peak, and late) and non-breeding periods. Lipid, protein, and ash components of each bird and of each crop gland phase were determined. Molt intensities of the body and primary wing feathers were not highly correlated with the protein reserves of the doves. Lipid reserves did not vary with sex, were highest for doves with active crop glands, and declined as the breeding season progressed. After adjusting for structural size differences, protein reserves were highest in doves with active crop glands and declined as the breeding season progressed. The ash component of females was highest for doves with developing/regressing crops and declined as the breeding season progressed. Our results suggest that Mourning Doves attempt to replenish nutrient reserves prior to breeding. Mourning Doves also may rely on the availability of nutritious foods to satisfy maintenance requirements. However, if the quantity and quality of food in a given area does not satisfy these requirements, body reserves may decline throughout the breeding season. Funding was provided by the Alabama Agricultural Experiment Station and Auburn University.

Factors Influencing Mourning Dove Nest Success in CRP Fields

JOHN P. HUGHES, U.S. Fish and Wildlife Service, P.O. Box 713, Canadian, TX 79014
ROBERT J. ROBEL, Division of Biology, Kansas State University, Manhattan, KS 66506
KENNETH E. KEMP, Department of Statistics, Kansas State University, Manhattan, KS 66506

Graduate student: John P. Hughes (M.S.); Project completed: May 1996

Mourning doves (*Zenaida macroura*) nest primarily in trees, and most research pertaining to nest success has dealt with wooded habitats. However, ground nesting is prevalent in the Great Plains, where mourning dove numbers have increased slightly since the mid-1980s when the Conservation Reserve Program (CRP) was initiated. We monitored mourning dove nest success in CRP fields in northeastern Kansas during 1994 and 1995 to determine if that habitat could be a source for the increased numbers. To determine relationships between mourning dove nest success and habitat characteristics, we measured field-level vegetation structure and surrounding landscape composition.

Vegetation measurements included vertical density, heights of live and dead vegetation, percent canopy covers of total, live, dead, grass, forb, and woody vegetation, percent litter cover, and litter depth. Landscape composition descriptors consisted of both edge habitat indices and land-use types within an 800-m radius of each CRP field. Edge habitat indices measured the extent of wooded edge vegetation and field edge-to-area ratio. Land-use types were cover-mapped into the following categories: cultivated (row crops and small grains), CRP, non-CRP grass (rangeland and hayfields), wooded, wetland, and residential.

A total of 90 mourning dove nests was used in nest success calculations. Daily nest survival rates did not differ between 1994 (0.9738; 95% CI 0.9600 - 0.9876) and 1995 (0.9583; 95% CI 0.9423 - 0.9743). Daily nest survival rates were not associated with either edge habitat or surrounding land-use, but were associated with three vegetation measurements. This relationship was described by the equation: [Mourning dove daily nest survival rate]$^{1/2}$ = 134.736 + 0.067(height of live vegetation) - 0.949(percent grass cover) - 1.083(percent live vegetation cover); $R^2 = 0.77$, $F_{3,11} = 12.075$, $P = 0.001$.

The results of our study show that mourning doves readily nest in CRP fields in northeastern Kansas, and that daily nest survival rates are influenced by field-level vegetation structure. For our study sites, an intermediate level of disturbance that provides low amounts of live vegetation and grass cover but high live vegetation height seems appropriate for mourning dove management. Mourning doves appear to prefer recently established grasslands having tall bunchgrass clumps with low basal area, and open areas between clumps. This pattern has been noted by other researchers (George et al. 1979), and may disappear as CRP fields age.

Financial support for this study was provided by the Kansas Agricultural Experiment Station (Contribution 99-518-J), the Division of Biology at Kansas State University, and the Max McGraw Wildlife Foundation.

Additional information can be obtained from: *Hughes, J.P., R.J. Robel, and K.E. Kemp. 2000. Factors influencing mourning dove nest success in CRP fields. Journal of Wildlife Management 64(4):1004-1008.*

Studies of Native Columbiformes in Tucson, Arizona

CLAIT E. BRAUN, Grouse Inc., 5572 North Ventana Vista Road, Tucson, AZ 85750

Expected Completion: December 2001

A pilot investigation of native columbids was initiated in a suburban area in Tucson, Arizona on 1 January 2000. Species being studied are: mourning dove (*Zenaida macroura*), white-winged dove (*Zenaida asiatica*), and Inca dove (*Columbina inca*). The objectives of the initial year of study were to: 1) describe the weight dynamics of AHY mourning doves in relation to molt progression and breeding status, 2) examine use of primary measurements as a tool to separate gender of mourning doves, 3) describe the weight dynamics of HY mourning doves by primary molt, and 4) investigate morphological measures as tools to assign gender to Inca and white-winged doves. Through 3 November 2000, 1,160 mourning doves, 93 white-winged doves, and 29 Inca doves were banded at one site with trapping being conducted one day each week (at least 4 days/month) starting in January 2000. Morphometric data were obtained for all birds newly banded as well as for all birds recaptured.

Preliminary data indicate mourning doves initiate breeding in January and continue some nesting activities into early September. HY mourning doves appear in trap samples in March with numbers steadily increasing through October. Body mass of AHY mourning doves appears to decrease with progression of the breeding season and increase post breeding. Based on measurements of wild-trapped mourning doves ($N = 1,160+$) and augmented by internal examination of gonads ($N = 100$) of AHY mourning doves harvested by hunters in southern Arizona, length of primaries 10 and 1 have promise to separate gender of mourning doves of all age classes.

Insufficient data were obtained on Inca and white-winged doves to draw meaningful conclusions. Additional hypotheses were developed for future testing on these two species. Plans for 2001 include continued banding of all three species and further testing of hypotheses including possible use of recapture data to examine population size and survival of mourning doves. This study is funded by Grouse Inc. and operates under permits from the U. S. Fish and Wildlife Service and the Arizona Department of Fish and Game. Check station data were obtained through coordination with the Arizona Department of Fish and Game.

www.ingramcontent.com/pod-product-compliance
Lightning Source LLC
Chambersburg PA
CBHW080738290526
45790CB00008B/3245